# RUN GREAT WHEN IT COUNTS: HIGH SCHOOL

## 31 TIPS TO RUN YOUR BEST AT THE END OF THE TRACK OR CROSS COUNTRY SEASON

JOEY KEILLOR

*Illustrated by Michael King*
*Cover Design and Layout by Patti Keillor and Paul Rohde*

ISBN-13: 978-1477649459

ISBN-10: 147764945X

First Edition

For additional copies or for discount bulk purchases of this book, contact Joey Keillor at www.rungreatwhenitcounts.com.

Run Great When It Counts: High School is intended to supplement individual advice from your coach. Specific health and medical advice contained within the book should not be acted on without consultation with your personal physician regarding your individual medical condition.

Cover Photo: Kraig Lungstrom.

*To high school cross-country, track and cross-country skiing coaches — such as Tom Morgan, Jeff Gullord, Jim Gulstrand and Peg Sorenson — who dedicate enormous amounts of time and energy to the betterment of youth, with little in the way of monetary compensation.*

# ≫🏹► | TABLE OF CONTENTS

 FORWARD

My greatest season of running ever was characterized by one key factor: improvement from beginning to end. I spent nine months as a sophomore at Mankato State University going from being a re-tread 10th man on the cross-country team to being the NCAA Division II national champion in the steeplechase.

That steeple was on the track at Emporia State University out on the prairies of Kansas. It had been a warm afternoon, but as the race neared, a thunderstorm blackened the sky and sent everyone scurrying for cover. The meet was postponed for an hour as the storm lashed the prairie and swept in a cool, dark air. Now it was night. The wet track glistened under the floodlights. We lined up and the gun went off. After one lap, I could just tell by how easy things felt that it was unlikely that anyone was going to beat me.

It was the most important race of the year. I felt great and ran great.

*After one lap, I could just tell by how easy things felt that it was unlikely that anyone was going to beat me. It was the most important race of the year. I felt great and ran great.*

Funny, though, how difficult this is to duplicate. In high school, my characteristic season started with good running and seemed to improve up to the conference meet where I usually ran my best. It went down from there, and I typically ran my worst race of the year at the Minnesota State Meet.

A similar pattern unfolded after my national championship year in college. A lot of hard work in the offseason made for about half of a good season, but then my mojo faded and mediocre to poor results followed. Luckily for me, mediocre still resulted in a ticket to the national meet on numerous occasions. Still, I'd trade any number of mediocre state or national meet appearances for one more top-level race feeling like I felt under the lights in Emporia, Kansas. I wouldn't even have to win: just give me the feeling of being at the top of my game when it counts most.

Enough about me, this is about you.

Regardless of your competitive level, your finishing time or how you place, I want you to run your best and feel your best at your most important race or races. Maybe this involves winning, maybe not. It's primarily about feeling great when you want to.

Even with the best planning and advice, this goal can still be elusive. There are no promises or guarantees.

Still, you can use the advice in this book to identify key factors that set the stage for success. It will help you to avoid the mistakes and flawed thinking that leads many talented high school athletes to have a season that begins with promise and ends with disappointment.

Moreover, when you learn what it takes to feel your best at the end of a long high school season, you'll be learning what it takes to run and feel good throughout the longest season of all: life.

*That's me, flying into the water pit in Long Beach, California during my first-ever steeple. Two months later, I was the NCAA Division II national champion.*

# ⟫**CC**► | INTRODUCTION

Do you find that during the last few races of the year:

* Your race performance doesn't match the level of your hard training?
* You've lost your usual zip at the end of races, and instead feel flat or out of shape?
* Your legs feel heavy or slow?
* You're finishing behind kids you've been beating or been competitive with for much of the season?
* You're running no faster and perhaps even slower than you did earlier in the year…and it feels harder?

If so, this book is for you.

But even if you usually do great at the end of the season, the advice in this book can help you avoid the pitfalls that can sometimes creep up on successful athletes.

First, let's come to an understanding. This book isn't a comprehensive guide to distance running. That's for two main reasons:

1. We're narrowing our focus to a certain problem and eliminating information that will distract you from addressing this problem.

2. If you're in a public or private high school and run for the cross-country or track team, you already have a coach who can give you a lot of advice and who will be formulating many of the details of your training program.

Therefore, this book tackles issues that may not be addressed by your high school coaches. Also, in terms of training, it offers instruction in how to approach the training your coach gives you — not instruction in what type of training to do.

This book isn't intended to replace your coach. It's meant to supplement your coach's guidance by giving you more knowledge about how you can control your body.

Repeated lackluster-to-downright-bad races at season's end probably isn't just bad luck. There's something wrong. It could be a health issue. It could be your own flawed thinking and misconceptions. It could be that your coach has a methodology that isn't working for you. Whatever the problem, you may need to assess what's not working — and take action to address it. This book will guide you in this process.

## LET'S GET STARTED!

When things aren't going well with training or racing, we Americans — with our consumer-driven mindset — have a hard time resisting the urge to find a product that will solve the problem. When I first start advising a new client (who has probably sought me out because things aren't going all that great), I'm usually asked what I think about some type of product. It could be the Vibram foot gloves, a vitamin supplement, knee-length compression socks or gluten-free food. Will these help me run better?

Well, maybe. Or maybe not. Certainly there are fairly specific problems that specific products can help solve. For example, a gluten-free diet is imperative for someone diagnosed with celiac disease. A foot glove or other minimalist footwear may help someone with low-back pain run pain-free. But declines in performance at the tail end of a season aren't going to be averted by a product that's just supposed to generally improve performance.

## SO WHAT WILL HELP?

The following 31 tips for running great at the end of the season are all related to four factors that are the underpinnings of successful racing: running, confidence, health, and talent. When you direct most of your focus and energy on understanding, leveraging or shoring up these factors it will yield the greatest result in terms of athletic improvement.

# PART I | RUNNING

If you want to be a good runner, you've got to run, run fast at least some of the time and probably do at least some supportive exercises. In addition, to improve over time, you'll need to gradually work over many seasons toward running more, running faster or both.

*But there's a catch:* you have to do this in a way that is sustainable and doesn't try to force fitness upon yourself. If you're a motivated teen, this probably means training that's less extreme than you think is necessary. The old adage "train, don't strain" is as true today as it's ever been. In contrast, the old adage "give 110%, expect 110%" just doesn't work for distance runners (and isn't mathematically possible, as far as I can tell).

The following tips revolve around the idea of nudging your training along (as opposed to pushing it) in a way that doesn't wear you out, that leads to progressive improvement and simply feels good.

# TIP #1: RUN MOST DAYS

It sounds too basic, but one common factor of training that isn't working very well is a lack of focus on the fundamentals. When it comes to running well, running is about as fundamental as it gets.

In short, you'll need to run most days of the year (unless you're in another sport or sports). About 265 days of running a year is good baseline benchmark for dedicated junior or senior high school runners. This allows you to take a three-week break in December, a three-week break in June, one day off each week, and about 12 spare days to rest when ill, injured or feeling really beat up or worn out.

*If you don't run most days of the year, it will be really tough to beat someone of similar (or even lesser) talent who does.*

If your only sports are track and cross-country, running during the official season isn't enough to realize your potential. Summer and winter off-season running is necessary. Running most days may be less achievable for freshmen or beginning runners, but should be increasingly do-able as you mature through your sophomore to senior year or with each year of added experience.

If you don't run most days of the year (or don't participate in other sports), it will be really tough to beat someone of similar (or even lesser) talent who does. In addition, if your training plan doesn't include running on most days of the year, it's probably not as good as it could be.

## HOW MUCH MILEAGE SHOULD I RUN?

There's no "right" answer to this question, but here are two truisms:

1. One major aspect of improving your running is to gradually increase the amount of mileage you can run, whether over a season, a year or many years

2. Everyone has a point of diminishing returns, where more mileage doesn't help and may begin to lead to worse results or cause injury.

A good place to start in determining an appropriate mileage is to choose a distance that you know you could handle if you ran that distance every day. This may be 1 or 2 miles for a beginner or five or more miles for a more experienced athlete. You don't necessarily have to run that distance every day (although doing so for two weeks would be a good test of your estimate). However, it gives you a mental framework for choosing a starting level, which you can gradually increase over time (see Tip#2).

How much is too much? There are many factors that can affect your "point of diminishing returns" so that at a certain mileage level, you may not benefit from raising your mileage — or may even need to lower it. Some of these factors include:

* Going from low-intensity off-season training to high-intensity training and racing in-season. You may need to hold your mileage steady or even lower it.

* Being active and busy, whether with homework, another sport, having a job or other activities. The busier you are, the less energy your body will have to recover from increased running volume.

* Feeling like you've reached a good level and not wanting to increase it.

* Your running history. Your body may struggle to handle a dramatic increase in mileage over what you've done in the past year ("dramatic" would mean adding more than about 10 miles per week on a routine basis over what you did the previous year).

Even if you have the time, energy and motivation to run a lot, a top end of about 60 to 70 miles a week is likely sufficient to achieve most high school running goals. Many goals can be achieved on less.

# TIP #2: START EASY AND GRADUALLY INCREASE

Injury, illness and fatigue have ruined many a season. Injury and illness can knock you out from the most important races of the year, or cause a gap in your training that can't be made up. Fatigue can result in stagnation and decline in performance during a long season.

One of the best ways to prevent illness, injury or fatigue in any physical activity is to start easy and gradually increase effort. This is the basic idea of adaptation. Your body experiences a new stress and, so long as you can recover from this stress, your body will adapt and improve its ability to handle it — and even thrive off of it! This seems so obvious, but this principle is categorically ignored by legions of runners (including myself, sometimes).

> *You can't rush fitness or athletic development. When you try, you're more likely to get hurt or fatigued, then experience declines in performance.*

One main reason for this, I believe, is that you can ignore this principle very successfully in the short term. Fit teenagers can really pound their body with intense physical activity — for several days or even consistently for several weeks — and seemingly suffer few ill effects.

The body has an amazing ability to go into temporary "overdrive" to handle sudden, intense changes in stress and activity. However, it also has a wide variety of mechanisms — such as fatigue, injury and illness — to bring prolonged "overdrive" activity to a slow-down or halt.

This phenomenon can sometimes be observed in newcomers to the track or cross-country team. On occasion, a newcomer goes all-out in the first days or weeks of the season. In almost every instance, this person sees a brief window of glory, followed by a steep, downward slide to poor performance or even to quitting the team — perhaps with a stop or two at the trainer's room along the way.

The phenomenon may be less obvious, however, when it occurs in slow motion. A good portion of runners who do well early in a season then stagnate or decline towards the season's end are probably going harder than the body is ready for early in the season, and doing so with inadequate rest and recovery.

This may be particularly true for athletes who do minimal off-season running, then launch into the regular season. It may also occur in fit athletes who train commendably in the off-season, then launch into the regular season with overly intense and amazing workouts and races. It may take a couple of weeks to a month or more of overtraining before you begin to notice stagnation, diminished performance, a consistent feeling of fatigue — or some sort of bodily breakdown.

The main point is that you can't rush fitness or athletic development. When you try, you're more likely to get hurt, ill or fatigued — and then experience declines in performance.

## DETERMINING HOW TO START "EASY"

**Week-to-week mileage:** When it comes to the amount of mileage you should run, Tip #1 can help you determine a starting point for your mileage goals. After you select a beginning mileage level, I suggest running at that level for two to three weeks. If you're feeling good and well-adapted to your beginning mileage level, you can choose to raise your mileage level (See Tip #15 for an alternate way to go about this).

A 10% rise in mileage over a level you've adapted to is often considered a good target, although a little more or less than that is o.k., too. Experienced runners can often ramp up more quickly to a manageable mileage level (based on past experience), and then increase more gradually after that. Ten percent increases may not sound like much, but when done consistently over time, it can add up to some serious mileage.

| 10% MILEAGE INCREASES OVER 10 WEEKS | | | | |
|---|---|---|---|---|
| Weeks 1-2 | Weeks 3-4 | Weeks 5-6 | Weeks 7-8 | Weeks 9-10 |
| Easy daily jogging to get your legs ready | 20 mpw* | 22 mpw | 25 mpw | 28 mpw |
| | 30 mpw | 33 mpw | 36 mpw | 40 mpw |
| | 40 mpw | 44 mpw | 48 mpw | 53 mpw |

*Miles per week (mpw)

**Year-to-year mileage:** For mileage increases from one year to the next, adding 5 to 10 miles a week over what you did the previous year is often considered a manageable (but not always necessary) increase. Of course, the exact amount you run week-to-week will vary throughout the year, so you'll have to make some honest, off-season and in-season estimates.

For example, if you top-out at running numerous 30-mile weeks during the summer off-season — and feel pretty good about it — you may consider upping that to running numerous 35 to 40 mile weeks during the summer of the next year. Maybe that doesn't seem like a lot, but after three years of following this guideline, you'll be running numerous weeks of 45 to 60 miles during the summer off-season.

One key benefit of gradually adding mileage — whether over weeks or years — is that you can adapt so that you're running at a similar intensity level as you did while running lower mileage amounts. The quality of your running stays roughly the same, but you spend more time (or miles) running at that quality level.

Making more dramatic increases in mileage isn't necessarily wrong for reasonably experienced runners. Some athletes experience a surge in motivation or discover at a certain point that running mileage is really their strong suit.

Just keep in mind that it can take a long time for the fruits of rapid mileage increases to emerge as the body usually struggles to adapt to any major increase in physical activity. This struggle may not manifest itself in injury or serious fatigue (because most people will naturally reduce intensity), but you may not see much improvement in race results for many months — or possibly a year or more.

A great example of this is that college freshmen often struggle to run times equal to what they ran in high school. This is at least in part because their bodies are scrambling to adapt to the suddenly higher levels of college-level training.

**Intensity:** With intense workouts such as intervals, it's much harder to quantify what counts as starting easy and gradually improving. You'll have to do this by feel.

When you first start doing more intense workouts, try holding back to the extent that you don't feel like you're doing enough. You should be thinking: "I can go harder" or "I can do more." I recommend doing this for the first one or two weeks that you begin more intense workouts.

For most, this will mean really holding back for the first one to two weeks of official track or cross-country practice. Holding back means you may be running behind similarly fit teammates or competitors at first. That can be hard to do. But the goal is to be running your best at the end of the season, and letting your body gradually adjust and adapt to harder training early in the season is part of this process.

After one to two weeks of under-doing-it with intensity level, you may be ready to advance to more of a 4/5ths effort level, where your intense workouts become harder but still remain within the upper end of the comfort zone (See Tip #16). Whether you further increase your intensity level during workouts as the season progresses depends on the approach you take to your training (See Tip #7).

It takes discipline and patience to start at a level you can handle and gradually increase, and you can get a better idea of the psychology of doing this by being like Jason Albers (See Tip #3).

# TIP #3: WHEN YOU THINK OF DAILY TRAINING, THINK OF JASON ALBERS

Who the heck is Jason Albers? Well, when I was in eighth grade shop (industrial arts), one extra credit project was making a ring out of a quarter. The project required patience, dedication and commitment, none of which are hallmark traits of most eighth graders — unless you are Jason Albers.

I met Jason Albers in kindergarten and knew him through graduation. In all that time, Albers never didn't smile. In Cub Scouts, we begged him to frown — just once — and he couldn't do it. He was a happy, positive, patient person of whom you couldn't speak badly unless you were telling lies.

To make a ring out of a quarter, we first found quarters with our birth year on it. Then, we "borrowed" metal spoons from the cafeteria. Over the course of several weeks, we struck the edge of the quarters thousands of times with the back of the spoon. Throughout the halls and classrooms of Westwood Junior High, you could hear the "tink, tink, tink" of metal on metal. Rules were made to stop us from hitting them. Everyone in the cafeteria ate their soup with forks since the spoons were all gone. Still, we tapped the quarters with amazing results.

Every tap made a tiny, almost imperceptible dent in the quarter. After a thousand taps, we could see that the edge of the quarter was getting smoother. A couple thousand more, and we could see the edge start to splay outward. Thousands more, and the edge of the quarter was as wide as a typical men's wedding ring. The date on the quarter splayed to the underside of the smooth, shiny outer surface.

*Think of a daily training session as a spoon tap on the edge of the quarter. It's many solid, quality spoon taps over a long period of time that make for elegantly rounded, smoothly polished performance.*

When the tapping was complete, we selected a metal drill bit that was a slightly larger circumference than our fingers. With the quarter clamped in place on the drill press, we bored a hole through the middle. After a little filing and sanding to smooth the rough edges, we had an attractive ring with our birth year on the underside.

Needless to say, Jason Albers made the best ring in the class. And he still has it!

Then there was Jason Miller. He was the anti-Albers, and after a few days of tapping his quarter with a spoon, he sought a faster way to get the job done. Miller put his quarter in a vice and hit the edge with a hammer. The metal splayed out in the same way, but the outer surface was dented and jagged, with an edge so sharp that it could take your finger off. Still, it was finished in two class periods and Jason Miller had his ring.

It's hard to stay motivated when results are slow to emerge and don't happen in obvious ways. This is why many people end up training the Jason Miller way. This way involves hammer hits of training as you seek to pound your way into better fitness.

Some people may use Jason Miller training as a way to make up for lost time, whether getting up to speed because of missed off-season training or when coming back from an injury. Even diligent, dedicated runners use Jason Miller training simply on the idea that you need to train hard to race hard. You may think, "How can I push myself to the limits in the big race if I don't push myself to the limits in practice?"

Jason Miller training can work for some people, especially if used in a limited and precise manner. For just about anyone, it can lead to good short-term results, such as running well early- to mid-season. However, when it comes to top end-of-season performance, frequently hammering out Jason Miller-style training is more likely to lead to rough and jagged results from a battered body — especially when combined with lots of hard racing.

When it comes to training for distance running, I would recommend that most high school athletes do it the Jason Albers way. Think of a daily training session as a spoon tap on the edge of the quarter. No one tap has to be incredibly hard or of any great importance. It's many solid, quality spoon taps over a long period of time that make for elegantly rounded, smoothly polished performance.

You may not notice advancement on a day-to-day basis, but when you look at the results of weeks to months of work, you realize that progress has been made and you're better than you were when you started.

Minimizing or eliminating Jason Miller-like hammering not only leaves you feeling less pummeled at the end of the season, you feel less pounded on a daily basis. Training is likely to feel good and leave you feeling fitter and stronger rather than doubled-over and wobbly-legged at the end of a session. You're much more likely to feel happy about your training (rather than dreading it), which will put a smile on your face. And as much as anything, this is the true Jason Albers way.

# TIP #4: LEARN TO DIFFERENTIATE TRAINING FROM STRAINING

On a bad day, it's easy to tell the difference between training and straining. After a warm-up, it's usually fairly early in the run or workout that you feel yourself struggling to run a pace that should feel fairly easy. If this happens to you, stop yourself from making a bad situation worse. Instead, relax and throttle back to an easy, enjoyable jog — or just jog or walk home. No big deal. Try again another day.

On a good day, differentiating "training" from "straining" can be more difficult and can take a lot of trial-and-error practice. On a good day, for me, it's like a switch. I'm cruising along doing a workout, working fairly hard but feeling good, then rather quickly the effort starts to feel much harder — perhaps my leg muscles start to feel a little like jello, the arms start to tingle or my stride tightens up — even though I haven't really changed anything. Then I start having to "strain" to do what I had previously been doing without straining.

This can happen with a steady run or with intervals. But you can (and should) do whole workouts without ever feeling strained — and you don't need to reach a strain level to call it a successful workout.

You're not going to know where the "strain" line is until you cross it. Fortunately, you can cross the line and strain for short periods of time and suffer few ill effects. It's probably even beneficial. It's when you keep struggling for a long time through a strained effort or when you repeatedly strain in workouts that trouble begins brewing.

You don't need to fear straining. Learn to develop an awareness of when it's happening and make rational training decisions to deal with it. The main choices include:

* **Throttle back a little and focus on relaxing.** You may find that you don't slow down when you make a conscious decision to decrease effort and relax.

* **Stop or dramatically slow to catch your breath.** Re-start your run slowly and let the best pace gradually come to you. Or, end the more challenging part of your workout while you're still feeling good and call it a day.

* **Fight through it, but expect that you may feel more fatigued than usual over the following two to three days.** Then, make appropriate training choices based on this expected fatigue (i.e. take it easy).

# TIP #5: KEEP YOUR WATCH AT "ARM'S LENGTH"

Intensity is a tricky concept because it's difficult if not impossible to accurately measure intensity, and the terms we use to describe intensity are subjective and open to a wide range of interpretation. For example, what does running "hard" mean? How do you measure it? How will you feel?

Just about any measuring device related to exercise — wristwatches, heart rate monitors, GPS devices — can have a use, but they also all have flaws.

Heart rate monitors are used in an attempt to measure effort or to measure for signs of fatigue. The idea here is that the pace that your heart beats indicates how hard your body is working. Data

*Your brain is the best device around. Learn to listen to your body and be honest with yourself or your coach about how you feel.*

can be used, in theory, to push yourself harder or back off because you appear to be going too hard. At rest, a heart rate that is elevated over your typical "resting heart rate" may indicate that your body isn't fully recovered and may not be ready for maximal exercise.

The GPS monitoring devices have added a new layer of accuracy to measuring effort, although they're not as accurate as most people think. You can measure distances travelled, pace, elevation gain and loss — and you can compare these results to past performance with fancy computer graphs that combine this information with heart rate data.

At a more expensive and time-consuming level, athletes use devices to prick their skin, obtain a blood sample and test that sample for lactic acid accumulation. The idea here is that lactate accumulation is an indicator of a certain level of strenuous exercise.

In most ways, these devices aren't necessary. You can be certain that there is some kid your age in Kenya or Ethiopia who has none of these devices and is a lot faster than you are.

Of course, any tool can have a use. GPS monitors can be a great way to do measured interval work away from the track. A heart rate monitor can give helpful feedback for someone who doesn't know much about how his or her body responds to exercise. It can also give some indication of exercise effort or recovery between intervals — and is often best used to hold you back from going too hard. A simple wristwatch can help you measure time spent running and can tell you your pace, which are both useful.

However, there are just as many ways that these devices can steer you in the wrong direction. Heart rate monitors and lactate testing only give you a measurement of one variable of a complicated and poorly understood mechanism — namely, how the body operates during exercise.

Let's say you feel crummy, your legs are dead and you can't get your heart rate up into a certain desired target zone. Do you then struggle harder to get your heart rate up so you can train effectively? I wouldn't recommend it.

Blood lactate testing can be unreliable because it's hard to calibrate and the exact role lactic acid plays in stressful exercise isn't fully understood. Is it a fuel? Is it the cause of fatigue or the result? Is it something else? Believe it or not, the answers to these basic questions aren't known.

Even the lowly wristwatch can be the source of unnecessary angst. The main reason is the emotional attachment so many of us have to "hitting certain splits." Here are a few examples of helpful and unhelpful ways to use a wristwatch:

| EXAMPLE #1 | You're running a 400-meter interval and your legs feel bad, you aren't breathing well and you're running like garbage. Your 400 meter split is 5 seconds slower than you wanted it to be. |
|---|---|
| Unhelpful | Arrgh! I'm so frustrated. My split sucked. I'm out of shape. All right, I'm going to go harder and get that split if it kills me! |
| Helpful | Fewfta, that stunk! Oh well, I feel like garbage and my time was slow. I must be fatigued. I'll just do a little jogging, call it a day and try again tomorrow. |

| EXAMPLE #2 | You're running a 400-meter interval and it's really windy on the backstretch. You feel good and are running at an appropriate level, but your time is 3 seconds off of what you wanted. |
|---|---|
| Unhelpful | All right, don't let the wind be an excuse. Let's really charge into it this time and nail that split! |
| Helpful | Wow, that wind is strong! Looks like it's taking a few seconds off of my usual time. I'll set the time I just ran as my benchmark for today and work off of that. |

**Summary:** Your brain is the best device around. You can use whatever device you want — I use a wristwatch — but don't rely on them alone to tell you how you feel because they don't know. A device only measures one aspect of what you or your body is doing. This can be helpful, but it's not a substitute for learning to listen to your body and being honest with yourself or your coach about how you feel. In addition, don't let a device drive your emotions — keep it at "arm's length."

## BONUS TIP: RACE TO COMPETE, NOT FOR TIME

In track — and to a lesser extent in cross-country — time is a big deal, and rightfully so. Everyone wants a personal best or record. However, when it comes to running your best at the end of the season, you should generally ignore the clock when racing.

Instead, run to compete, and the fast times will come.

A classic scenario when running for an ambitious time is that you begin a race — a mile, let's say — with 200 or 400 meter splits in your mind. You set off in the race and hit your first split a couple of seconds behind plan. You immediately surge so that you hit your next split on time. By half way, you're back on schedule, but feeling a little tired. Still, you know you have to keep pushing to stay on pace.

You reach 1200 meters and are straining, only to find that you're down two seconds from your goal split. You strain through the backstretch, and suddenly kids start flying by with their finishing kick. Not only do you not win the race, but you don't get your goal time. And funny enough, the kid who won the race did get your goal time…even though he or she was way behind you for most of the race.

Racing against the clock can work in certain settings. It may also be a helpful tool to slow you down in the early part of a race if you tend to go out too fast. Still, most of the time, racing against the clock is frustrating and doesn't lead to the desired result. In contrast, when you compete with those around you, you:

* Can run easier in a less competitive race and not wear yourself out.

* May be able to throttle back mid-race, waiting to unleash with a kick.

* May push yourself to run faster than you thought possible because you don't let a fast split time intimidate you into slowing down.

* Have more fun (that is, assuming you find competition fun).

And guess what? If you run to compete, you'll eventually be in a race in which the competition will push you to your maximum, and the great time that you wished you could run will happen. Let it.

# TIP #6: RECONSIDER WHAT "HARD" TRAINING MEANS

Ask around. Ask different runners to define what "hard" means in terms of running. Some people might think intervals are hard, in the sense that they cause intense discomfort. Others may find running a long distance hard, as the discomfort tends to be more widespread and deep-seated. Still others may define hard running as going until you feel like puking or passing out, giving it all that you have.

While I agree that it's "hard" to run in a way that's intensely uncomfortable (and that this may sometimes be beneficial), I don't agree that running in this way defines what it means to "work hard" or "train hard."

I think the "hard work" of becoming a better distance runner is being consistent over long periods of time and having the discipline to gradually advance your ability to run farther and faster in a way that allows your body to adapt and thrive. For example, running 265 or more days a year is hard and most people can't (or don't) do it.

In addition, the discipline to train within yourself is one of the hardest skills to master. It's extremely tempting for good runners to run as hard as possible in every race of the season. It's hard to let teammates run faster than you in workouts. It can be satisfying to put newbies in their place by crushing them in a workout. It's a temptation to impress others with how fast you can run an interval or a fairly unimportant race. It's also difficult to recognize the staleness that can come from over-doing it and to take appropriate rest to remedy it (See Tip #8).

To me, consistent training over long periods of time, training within yourself and having the patience to let your body adapt to gradually harder training is much harder to do than going until you puke.

# TIP #7: STICK TO ONE MAJOR TRAINING APPROACH AT A TIME FOR IN-SEASON TRAINING

Tom Morgan, a high school coach of mine, had a saying: "You can't soar with the eagles in the day and fly with the owls at night." Although he mainly meant this as a way to suggest that you can't be horsing around all night and expect to perform during the day, it's also a truism of training.

There are two main variables of training: intensity and duration. Thinking of these two variables as dials or levers can help you understand how they can be used to manipulate your training. You can dial up, or dial down your intensity, and you can dial up or dial down your duration (or volume of running).

The two major types of training you're likely to encounter include:

1. Turning up the intensity dial and keeping the duration dial at medium or low. This would mean high speed running and workouts, with easy days as needed and lower volume

2. Turning up the duration dial and keeping intensity at medium or low. This would mean less intense workouts with more volume.

Although aspects of both approaches can be mixed and matched to a certain extent, simultaneously turning up the dials of both intensity and volume training is often a recipe for lackluster end-of-season performance — especially when done quickly

The reason that short bouts of fast, intense training with numerous easy days works is that the intensity is balanced with ample rest. The reason that longer, less-intense bouts of training works is that you can sufficiently recover by the next day — or do it for numerous consecutive days before taking an easier day. With either method, your next bout of training occurs when you are sufficiently recovered from the last.

However, when you simultaneously turn the dials of intensity and duration to a difficult level, it's very likely that the balance between work and recovery will be unequal, leading to fatigue, stagnation, poor performance, illness, injury or all of the above.

Many in-season high school distance training programs involve two to three "hard" days each week and four days of less intense running. If that's the way your team practices, try to stick to one of the two approaches below at any given time:

## APPROACH #1: GO AT HIGH SPEED OR HIGH INTENSITY, BUT DON'T CONCERN YOURSELF WITH MILEAGE GOALS

This involves working into a 90% to 98% effort on most of your hard days, and running non-taxing recovery miles on the easy days. You'll still need to start at a level you can handle and gradually improve (See Tip #2) and use the "train don't strain" ideas in Tip #4. Even if you're running at a 98% effort, you should still be composed, relaxed, feeling powerful and certainly not flailing.

The goal with this type of training is to run fast and feel good about it. Sure, you're winded at the end of an interval, but you're finishing strong and still have a spring in your step shortly after the workout is over. You can enhance its effectiveness by using the off-season — or a dedicated part of your regular season — to run higher volumes of less-intense mileage to gain the benefits of increased endurance.

A stumbling block is forcing yourself to run fast when you're already worn out, you're feeling flat or clunky, or your leg muscles start to feel like jello. An example is grinding out uncomfortable intervals after you've crossed the line between training and straining.

Also, the appropriate number of "easy" days you'll need to recover from a "hard" day can vary — especially if that "hard" day happens to be a race. It can take two, three or sometimes even more days of light training until you're ready to hit it hard again (see Tip #13).

On the other hand, if you're not killing yourself on the harder days, you may be able to do two or more harder days in a row before you feel the need for an "easy" day or days. I find that fast, intense workouts that are about one-half to three-quarters of what I'd consider full workout duration allow me to do this. In other words, I stop when I feel like I could do more...and the next day I can.

An astute reader may see a contradiction between this training method and the recommendations in Tip #3 on training the Jason Albers way. After all, isn't high-intensity training more like the Jason Miller hammer hits? Sure, maybe there's some difference, but I don't think it's an outright contradiction.

The Jason Miller way involves hammering your self to an exhausted pulp. Running at high speed doesn't have to be this way. To reiterate, the goal with this type of training is to run fast and challenge yourself, but also to feel good about it. If you're not feeling good about it, you may need to run a little less fast, run fewer intervals, run fewer overall miles, or take more recovery days.

## APPROACH #2: EMPHASIZE OVERALL MILEAGE (RELATIVE TO YOUR ABILITY AND PAST EXPERIENCE) AND 4/5THS EFFORT ON THE "HARD" DAYS

The goal here is to accumulate lots of minutes and hours running at a fast, comfortable pace (see Tip #16 on discovering your high-end comfort zone). In terms of mileage, you don't necessarily need to be racking up huge weeks, but you'll want the mileage level to feel challenging yet sustainable.

On the "hard" days, this training style would involve going at or less than a maximum 90% effort. This would mean working into an effort that is at — or maybe sometimes slightly above — your high-end comfort zone. A pitfall with this mode of training is going too hard on the "hard" days, so it's important to really feel within your comfort zone and to back off from your hardest effort level (See Tip #13). Don't mistake this for slow running. You can run fast intervals and still remain at or below a 90% effort level, especially if you practice running in that way.

Most — but probably not all — of the easy "recovery" days involve medium- to high-quality mileage within the high-end comfort zone. Again, this isn't jogging (unless you're having a bad day, in which case you should jog). For example, well-trained, varsity-level boys can run 6:00 per mile pace or faster for a good portion of a 5- to 10-mile run and still be within the comfort zone.

## WHAT'S BEST?

I feel that the majority of high school distance athletes will experience their best success using the 4/5ths effort level and higher mileage training approach. It satisfies the need to run high-quality mileage to improve, while diminishing the risk of over-doing it with high intensity. A unique aspect of high school competition that makes this more likely to work is the numerous races during the typical season. Frequent racing is your high-intensity training. Adding more in practice may not be necessary — or may even become counterproductive.

Still, I've run some great races training in a high-intensity, low-mileage way — and there are successful high school programs that do high-intensity, low-mileage training. However, a key risk is that it can be hard to avoid over-doing it with too much high intensity training — particularly when coupled by frequent racing. This may make it harder to run great at the end of the season without a very mature ability to listen to your body or without guidance from a knowledgeable coach who can keep you from "going to the well" too often.

## AVOID PAINFUL EXTREMES

Whatever method you and your coach choose the goal is to run fast in a way that feels good, rather than to routinely push your body to painful extremes. When you routinely train to painful extremes your body is unlikely to adapt, improve and thrive. In addition, you begin to associate fast running with pain, discomfort and strain. This may lead to dreading workouts or even an inability to relax in a race setting.

In contrast, feeling good and running fast leads to several positives related to enjoyment, such as wanting to run more, not fearing a fast pace, and having a positive, confident mindset. If your coach has you doing some kind of training that's different than the choices above, see Tip #12 for assurance that you can perform well under many kinds of training plans with the right approach.

## BONUS TIP: THE RACE VARIABLE

Racing can be a great component of training. But it's easy for high school distance runners to race too much.

Although hard to quantify, everyone has a "well" of racing energy with a limited amount of energy to draw upon. There's a limit to the number of all-out, high intensity races you can run in typical high school track or cross country season before the "well" begins to run dry and performance goes flat or starts to decline (but don't lose all hope if this happens to you...see Tip # 8). Not only does lots of high-intensity racing wear you down over time, it also crowds out time for ordinary training.

It's hard to put an exact number on what constitutes "too much." But if you're racing hard every week, it may be difficult for you to feel your best at the end of a 3-month season. If you race hard more often than that, it may become even more difficult to feel good late-season.

The two main ways you can avoid "going to the well" too often are to:

- **Talk to your coach about skipping certain meets** — Some people dislike this idea as it goes against the idea of team spirit. I would argue that the best thing for team spirit is to have the best runners firing on all cylinders at the end of the season. This may mean that some runners need to sit out certain races, just as no basketball player plays every minute of every game.

- **Talk to your coach about running at a lower intensity in certain races, such as a maximum of a 4/5ths effort** — Maybe you don't finish as high as you might ordinarily finish or run as fast, but the goal isn't to run great at every rinky-dink race, it's running great when it counts. In addition, running a 4/5ths effort at a meet can be a great workout and can help with your fitness development.

Many coaches incorporate these ideas into their race scheduling. If your coach doesn't, he or she may be receptive to your desire to save some mojo for the big races. Otherwise, you may need to take action on your own to maintain your reservoir of all-out energy for the important races. Steps might include:

- Running only as hard as necessary in low-key races (or as easy as possible, depending on how you think of it)

- Making sure to get enough rest days after races

- Avoiding "going to the well" in practice by making sure you run in a way that feels good and isn't breaking you down.

## A FINAL THOUGHT

It's true that in American running history, rare people like Steve Prefontaine, Pat Porter, Joan Benoit-Samuelson and others have been known for doing lots of incredibly hard workouts, multiple days in a row while simultaneously running fairly high to very high mileage. Similarly, many of the great Kenyan and Ethiopian athletes of the past two decades have been known for merging high volume with high intensity training.

But people who can thrive off of this type of training probably aren't very common. Indeed, for every great Kenyan runner, we don't see the hundreds or thousands of Kenyans who couldn't physically handle a "survival of the fittest" training regimen. Moreover, people who can do this are typically extremely talented adults who have built up to being able to do this over the span of many years (see Tip #2) — and they may not do much else throughout the day other than run and rest.

Closer to home, perhaps you have a teammate who can really hammer out workouts and races week after week and performs just great. Maybe it works for them — or maybe they aren't going as hard as you think or are getting more rest than you realize. Or, you may just be seeing a window of success that may not last over the longer term.

Aggressive training can play a role in success for some people, and is perhaps best used with limited precision. But it isn't necessarily better, especially when used as your full-time training philosophy.

Indeed, incredibly hard training has shot down far more people than it has benefitted. You can still attain high levels of success and not train so aggressively — at least while you're in high school and maybe even well beyond. It's all about doing the training that is best for your body, not what is best for someone else.

# TIP # 8: AVOID RESPONDING TO MID-SEASON FATIGUE AND PERFORMANCE DECLINES WITH HARDER TRAINING

Let's face it, it's tough to be Jason Albers and it's easy to get swept up into training and racing hard early in the season — especially if you have a fun, competitive group of teammates or if you're the "star" who always has to be great. In addition, it can be tough to know what's "too much." You may not know you went too hard until your body knocks you back with an injury, stagnation or persistent fatigue.

If you start to feel like you're stagnating or fatiguing — which may be indicated by having heavy or tight legs for more than a day or two, having to work harder in races or workouts to achieve your usual result, or by having actual declines in performance — you face an easy (though difficult to execute) decision.

I faced this decision my senior year of high school. I ran a fantastic 800-meter race at the conference meet, scarcely nipping the fleet-footed Pat Farley to win in 1:56. But at the section meet I felt flat. I struggled and strained to secure a qualifying place for state.

Naturally, I concluded the flat feeling was a sign that I wasn't training hard enough. In the remaining week to the state meet, I ran an extra hard interval workout to pound myself back into shape. The workout felt bad and I couldn't hit splits that ordinarily shouldn't have been that hard. At the state meet, I felt tight and slow. I got dusted in the preliminary and watched the final from the stands.

Unfortunately, many runners' respond to fatigue or performance declines in exactly the way that I did: by training harder. Other runners may just keep doing what they've been doing in the hopes that they'll freshen up.

If you're tiring out, if training or racing feels harder or performance is declining, the simple choice is to back off in your training. Depending on the extent of your fatigue, you may be fine doing something like 50% of normal until you start to feel better — or you may have to rest even more by just jogging a little each day until you start to feel better.

When you start feeling better, avoid the temptation to hyper-train to make up for lost time. Instead, get back into training at a notch or two below where you left off or training at a level that feels like you're not doing enough. Over the course of several sessions, you may be able to ramp back up to harder, but still manageable, training levels.

# TIP #9: DON'T RELY ON AN END-OF-SEASON TAPER FOR REJUVENATION

Here is a classic line that's been spoken about three-quarters of the way through many-a-season: "I'm tired now, but just wait until I taper."

But guess what? Instead of feeling rejuvenated when you taper, you run the most important end-of-the-year races feeling flat or stale — or maybe even weak or out of shape. Maybe you do o.k., but hardly your best. Maybe you have your worst race all season.

The traditional end-of-season taper consists of drastically diminished training — which often involves a switch to short, high-speed workouts or races or "sharpening." This type of taper is used a lot, but it isn't the sure-fire method of rejuvenation that it's often thought to be — particularly in a low-volume, high-intensity setting.

The problem with traditional tapering plans is usually one of two things:

* You weren't all that fatigued, and the taper causes you to lose fitness as you suddenly stop doing all of the things that got you to where you were before the taper started.

* You're too fatigued, your "well" of energy is pretty much dry, and a taper isn't enough to get you back to feeling good again. Then you also get out of shape due to lack of training, and that's when you're really messed up.

## NOT FATIGUED

Most high school athletes run volumes in the range of 20 to 50 miles a week. True, some may put up great off-season mileage, but during the season it's generally (and often wisely) back to these volumes due to the stresses racing and hard training efforts (not to mention other important uses of time and energy such as school work and social activities).

In this setting, cutting back on already moderate weekly mileage during a taper may negatively affect conditioning because you're doing too little exercise — especially if the taper lasts for more than a week as you prepare for the conference, section and state meet.

Even if you don't get out of shape, the idea of tapering by making your volume lower — and making the already fast speeds even faster — probably isn't going to do much to improve end-of-season performance. It would be akin to pushing the accelerator of your car to the carpet when it's already almost at the carpet.

## TOO FATIGUED

In this scenario, you spend weeks or months leading up to your big races training at an overly high level. Although this may have lead to good results early in the season, at some point, you go into a fatigue deficit.

You become fatigued enough so that your recovery days aren't enough to allow your body to get back to full strength. Still, you don't cut back on training or racing, and the fatigue deficit remains, possibly leading to workouts or races that feel harder than usual or even to declines in performance.

But never fear! As the big, end-of-season races approach, you rest up with a taper of drastically diminished training.

Many kids train and race in this way simply because that's a common way for a track or cross-country season play out. However, some people deliberately train this way on the belief that fitness will "super-compensate" or snap back from a fatigued state with such momentum that it goes above your usual level of fitness. Others simply feel that hard training is necessary, and that the benefits of that training will be fully revealed by rest.

Whatever the reason, I would recommend avoiding training yourself into a prolonged state of fatigue on the hope that a late-season taper will allow your body to rejuvenate — or even super-compensate.

It's very unlikely to yield better results than if you'd trained in a sustainable, progressive way — and there is a good chance that it will lead to worse results.

Many people get to a point in the season where running feels harder or the legs start to feel heavy or tight and they think to themselves: "I just have to get though the next couple weeks of hard training, then I can rest and taper."

If this happens to you, it's a warning sign. Don't keep grinding away toward a far-off taper. See tip #8 right away for ways to get your self back to full strength.

## WHAT'S THE ALTERNATIVE?

**First:** Avoid being so fatigued that you feel the need for a traditional taper. Your legs should never really feel tired for more than two or maybe three days at most (with the possible exception of longer fatigue after a hard race).

All of the tips in Part I: Running and also tips #13 and #16 will help you think about training in a way that emphasizes adaptation and gradually ramps up your volume and training speed in a way that feels good and makes you stronger. Also, Tip #7 offers two main approaches to in-season training that can get you to the end of the season without feeling fatigued.

**Second:** Re-think the nature of late-season training. Backing off some at the end of the season makes perfect sense (although it's not a requirement). But the traditional idea of dropping your mileage and doing brief, fast intervals is just one idea — and one that seems way over-used and under-proven.

Instead, think of the training that made you good earlier in the season. If you raced great off of that training (and didn't end up with a fatigue deficit), why would you suddenly shift to a totally different way of training in the last few weeks of the season? Take the training that made you good and just do, say, 25% or 50% less in volume or intensity in the days before a big race. See three examples in the chart below.

The goal is to provide good training stimulus, but without much — if any — fatigue. In addition, never force a workout during this time if it feels bad. Stop early or slow down. Relax. If you stop, try another moderate effort the next day.

| SUCCESSFUL MID-SEASON TRAINING | 75% OF WORKOUT | 50% OF WORKOUT |
|---|---|---|
| 8 x 400 meter in 66 seconds | 6 x 400 meter in 66 seconds | 4 x 400 meter in 66 seconds |
| | 12 x 200 meter in 33 seconds | 8 x 200 meter in 33 seconds |
| | 8 x 400m at a relaxed, 4/5ths pace | 6-8 x 400m at a relaxed, 4/5ths pace |
| 3 x 1-mile in 6 minutes each | 2 x 1-mile in 6 minutes | 1 mile in 6 minutes, followed by a half-mile in 3 minutes |
| | 5 x half-mile in 3 minutes each | 3 x half-mile in 3 minutes each |
| | 3 x 1-mile at a relaxed intensity such as running them in 6:15 or 6:30 | 2-3 x 1-mile at a relaxed intensity such as running them in 6:15 or 6:30 |
| Running 40 miles a week and doing one interval workout and one long run during the week | Lower your mileage to 25 miles, but keep the long run and the workout fairly intact, so long as they feel good | Lower your mileage to 20 miles, take just a little effort or distance off of the long run and the workout |

# TIP #10: KEEP YOUR EYES OPEN TO THE FACTS OF WHAT WORKS FOR YOU

Have you ever heard a fellow runner or a coach make a statement like this: "We're doing good now, but just wait until we start doing harder training!"

This is a classic line often spoken about one quarter to one third of the way through a cross-country or track season. It's usually spoken after a successful race off of "base" training (or training that involved lower intensities).

What usually follows are weeks or months of intense workouts and races. The funny thing is, subsequent races may be no better, and in some cases they may even be worse.

I'm not advocating that you do only base training or never train intensely or never increase your training. Many training strategies can play a role in success.

Rather, I want you to stay clear-eyed as to what works for you. Also, strive to avoid blanket acceptance of preconceived ideas of what's supposed to work. A season of hard, maximal efforts to "steel" yourself for hard racing is one such idea with a high rate of use, but with a low rate of success.

How can you know if training is working for you? Here are two ways:

* **Look at results** — Race results are often consistent indicators of what's working and what isn't. Running good times at mid-season and worse times (or place) at the end of the year usually isn't just bad luck (unless you have mitigating issues, such as a health problem). Sure, everyone has a bad race now and again, but lasting or repeated declines or stagnation indicate a need for change or adjustment.

* **Listen to how you feel** — Feeling flat, tired, heavy-legged, clunky, like you've lost your zip or are "in the hole" isn't good. Sure, you'll get days like this, maybe a couple days in a row even with optimal training. But that's about the max it should be. If your training is making you feel this way for more than a couple of days in a row, and you rule out a health problem, it's likely too hard, too much or just not right for you. Training should be nudging you upward toward a greater sense of feeling strong, powerful, fast and unstoppable. Choose more of the training that makes you feel this way.

# PART II │ CONFIDENCE

Confidence can take many forms. The most obvious is starting-line confidence where you feel like you've done an appropriate amount of work to prepare for a given race.

However, training confidence is equally, if not more, important. This is the ability to know how to — or when you've — put in an appropriate effort for the day. This means having the confidence to stop a training session at the right time, to run at a reasonable effort level, to not second-guess yourself or your coach and to realize that there isn't some secret that you don't know about.

Lack of training confidence leads to overtraining, overly hard running, undue focus on relatively unimportant factors — and a lot of unproductive worry.

# TIP #11: THERE ISN'T A SPECIAL TYPE OF TRAINING THAT YOU DON'T KNOW ABOUT

High school runners often doubt that they are doing the best possible training to improve as a runner. It's easy to succumb to the "grass is always greener on the other side" way of thinking. You may feel that your coach, teammates, school or town is inferior in some way to the town on the other side of the state that's continuously cleaning your clock.

It's easy to believe that people who run better than you when it counts are doing some sort of special training. Is it a certain running workout? A weight lifting regimen? A certain series of workouts over the season? If only you knew the secret.

In many ways, running isn't that complicated and you're probably doing more effective things than you realize. When it comes to specific workouts there are only a few ways to train, and none of them are a secret. They include:

- **Steady running of varying duration and effort level** — This includes "lactate threshold" running, which is usually defined as having a duration of about 15 to 30 minutes at roughly a 90% effort level. It also includes "tempo" running, which is of longer duration than a lactate threshold run and is done at an 80 to 85% effort level. A progression run is similar to a tempo run, except that the pace gradually increases throughout the run. Finally, continuous uphill running for 10 to 20 minutes or more can be done on a treadmill or on a long mountain road.

- **Intervals** — These can be longer for endurance, shorter for speed or uphill for strength. Speed-play (fartlek) running is intervals of faster or more intense running interspersed throughout a steady run.

- **Slower running** — This is used for recovery or for getting back into shape following a break. It can also be beneficial if you are running a long way, running longer than usual, or greatly expanding the amount of mileage you're running over the long term.

- **Race or time trial** — This is approaching a 95 to 100% effort level, metered out over the full distance of the race. This may include a competitive element or a focus on "holding it together" in the face of discomfort.

There you have it. All of distance running in about 200 words. The best runners in the world — or even your cross-state rival — don't do anything different from what is listed above.

When it comes to having confidence in how you train, you can start by having confidence that there isn't a special type of training that you don't know about. In fact, these types of training have been used since the 1960s and, in most cases, for much longer than that. Not much has changed in 50 years and it's unlikely that things will change much in the future.

# TIP #12: YOU CAN RUN YOUR BEST OFF OF A VARIETY OF TRAINING PLANS

O.K., so what if you have all of the pieces of the puzzle. How do you put that puzzle together?

There are a lot of good training plans out there. For most high school runners, a coach devises their training plan and it's usually performed as group training with teammates.

Where does your coach get a plan? Coaching certifications require studying training ideas for distance runners. Many coaches are runners or former runners, and have a good idea of what constitutes a good training plan. Coaches also learn from experience what works best. In addition, many running books and Internet sites contain sample plans.

A few common and totally legitimate training plans include:

## PERIODIZED TRAINING

The idea of periodization is most closely associated with Arthur Lydiard, the great New Zealand coach of the 1950s and 1960s.

Classic periodization involves three phases typically over, a four- to six-month period of time. These include building a base of high-mileage over a period of months, a transition period focusing on hill training, and a final "sharpening" phase of daily interval work of varying lengths and intensities, and time trials.

Some coaches attempt to follow some sort of periodized schedule, but it's mostly impossible to follow a true Lydiard-style system within the time frame of a typical track or cross-country season schedule.

There's no time for the base building phase (unless athletes do this on their own in the summer or winter off-season), the hill phase may be condensed to a few sporadic workouts, and the majority of the season is spent in the "sharpening" phase doing hard bouts of training and racing, followed by one to three days of rest.

Moreover, the Lydiard sharpening phase involved near-daily interval sessions or time trials, which most teams don't do.

## TOUCH ALL THE BASES TRAINING

This involves touching on the major categories of training throughout the week. You may do a long run, a hill session and an interval session all in the same week. Of course, there are also the slow days and races shuffled into the mix.

## EXTENSION TRAINING

This is often associated with Italian endurance coaches. The idea is to first develop your ability to move your feet and run at a fast, pace over shorter, manageable distances. Over the course of the season, you extend the distance at which you can run a fast, manageable pace.

This general methodology is probably used a lot — whether on purpose or by default — and it's probably mixed with "touch all the bases" training. Basically, you're doing a few different workouts early in the season, and those gradually increase in difficulty as the season progresses.

## SO WHICH PLAN IS THE BEST?

Guess what? Nobody knows! That's because it's likely impossible to prove scientifically that any sort of training program is superior to any other.

A scientific study to determine a better program would require large groups of people doing the same training program, and comparing this group to another large group who did another training program. Even if this were possible, it would be extremely difficult to know which variable or variables from the two training programs was responsible for any difference in performance.

*What sometimes gets lost in the quest for the perfect plan is the importance of the approach to the plan.*

Still, some coaches and some athletes just seem to be better at being ready at the right time than do others — somebody must know something.

But is it really the training plan that's responsible for success?

Probably not. Among high school coaches who have had a long record of success, you'll find a wide variety of philosophies and training plans. This includes the plans mentioned above, but could also include such extremes as doing intervals every day, or only running mileage and never doing a high-intensity workout — or just about anything in between.

What sometimes gets lost in the quest for the perfect plan is the importance of the approach to the plan. When you approach a plan properly — by effectively controlling the amounts of volume and level of intensity that you run — the intricate details become less crucial.

In fact, you don't want to let over-attention to details cause worry or damage your confidence. You want to build confidence knowing that you and your coach can control your approach to whatever plan you have developed.

Examples of ways to control your approach abound in Part I: Running. They include starting at a level that you can handle and gradually improving (Tip #2), minimizing straining (Tip #4), not struggling against your body (Tip #5), avoiding the need for a big taper (Tip #9) and choosing one type of in-season training at a time, whether it's fast, lower volume running, or higher volume running at a 4/5ths intensity level (Tip #7).

A key point in all of this advice is that your daily training — though challenging — shouldn't leave you feeling totally trashed, jello-legged or worn out (See Tip #13 on how to back off).

When you can train at a challenging level that isn't totally breaking you down, you are training in a way that allows your body to adapt and thrive. When this happens, you can have confidence that you'll get better, no matter what training plan you adopt.

# TIP #13: HAVE THE CONFIDENCE TO BACK OFF

For coaches with motivated, hard-working runners, the task of coaching is usually more about pulling on the reins rather than cracking the whip. This can be especially true when you have a competitive team dynamic.

It can be really tricky for your coach. Your coach may not be able to tell when your body is asking you to go easier or rest. Or, you may not listen to your coach who pleads with you to take it easy.

However it happens, training too hard and too much is universal path towards stagnation or decline in the latter half of the season. The main reason is that you need to train in a way that allows your body to adapt. Training too hard and too much essentially means that your body can't keep up with the increased amount of physical stress. Instead of adapting and thriving, your body gradually starts going into survival mode and seeks ways to shut you down so it can get the rest it needs.

Even if you have the greatest coach in the world, athletes themselves bear a fair amount of responsibility in determining when they need to back off. Only you know how you feel. Others can only speculate based on what you say, how you look or how you perform.

The trouble is that it can be hard to know when you're going too hard. This is a primary conundrum for runners at all levels, as the drive to be your best clouds over signals that your body sends.

Another complication is that fatigue doesn't always have a clear cause-and-effect relationship to what you have done. You may be able to go too hard for two weeks before fatigue catches up, at which point you wonder why you're suddenly feeling worn out when you haven't done anything different for the past few days.

*You may find that you get equal fitness benefit from backing off as you would from pushing hard — and you won't pound your body as much.*

I don't have all of the answers for how to work hard enough without overdoing it, but a few thoughts on the following page can help you understand when it may be best to back off. These are very challenging decisions to make and many athletes don't have the confidence to make them.

If you are a hard-working runner motivated to do everything you can to be your best, I would urge you to at least experiment with making a decision to back off — particularly when you're feeling good in training. If you do, try to make an honest evaluation of whether it seemed to help. In fact, this may be a tricky evaluation because backing off may not directly make you better.

However, you may find that you get equal fitness benefit from backing off as you would from pushing hard — and you won't pound your body as much. Therefore, the long-term risk of injury or fatigue-related stagnation and decline are much lower.

Backing off may include minor adjustments such as running a little less weekly mileage or taking the intensity of your harder runs down a notch. Backing off may also involve taking a few days off or skipping a few hard workouts or a race. Consider backing off if:

- **You're feeling dead-legged, slower than normal, fatigued or tired for more than a couple of days a week** — If this occurs, you may need to change something in your overall training routine, including running less, running at a lower effort level, getting more sleep, or potentially seeing a doctor. Training and running should feel good most of the time.

- **After an appropriate warm-up, your legs feel dead or you're struggling to run a pace that shouldn't be that difficult (whether a long run, steady run or interval)** — If this occurs, STOP. Jog back to school or back home. Stretch a little. Maybe do some self-massage such as with a foam roller. Relax, and realize that everyone has off days. Come back and try again the next day.

  Dead legs are a different problem than sore muscles. You can often run pretty good on sore muscles. The key distinction that you should be paying attention to is having a heavy, clunky feel to your legs and struggling to run at a pace that ordinarily wouldn't be a struggle.

- **You're feeling somewhat "off," but not terrible, early in a run**— Some days, after warming up, you start running and you don't feel lousy enough to give up, but you don't feel all that great either. These are great days to dial back your effort level early in the run. Continually remind yourself to stay a notch below the speed you think you could be running.

  Backing off the effort helps your body relax and can help you ease into the run. You may never feel great — but by gently letting the pace come to your legs, you'll often end up running faster than if you were trying to run a quicker pace. The goal of a run like this is to feel better at the end of the run than you did early in the run. Sometimes, backing off a little early on gives your body a chance to wake up and you end up feeling great.

- **You feel great** — Sometimes (and maybe even most or all of the time) it may be best to back off and NOT push yourself to the maximum when you're feeling good in training. An 80 to 90% effort on a "hard" training day is a fantastic — and perhaps optimal — top-end goal.

Another goal is to avoid feeling "trashed," wobbly-legged or totally depleted after a workout. Maximal efforts can have a role in training, but high school runners who race a lot (which is most of them) probably get a sufficient number of maximum efforts at races. There may be little need for additional maximum efforts in practice. It may even be necessary to back off in — or skip — a few races to avoid going "to the well" too often.

If you have a hard workout coming up, try running it at a level that's a solid notch below maximal. Throughout the workout, continually ask yourself: Am I relaxed? Could I run faster? Could I do more? If you can answer "Yes" to those questions throughout an entire workout, you're probably running at a level that is incredibly beneficial and likely to leave you feeling bouncy and energized at the end, rather than trashed.

## BONUS TIP: MINIMIZE RACING IN PRACTICE

Many people love track and cross country because they're competitive, driven athletes. These can be great — perhaps essential — qualities. But being competitive and driven can work against you when you overuse these skills in practice.

The classic scenario involves a group of teammates who agree to go for a 5-mile run at a moderate pace. The pace starts modest enough, but then someone is feeling good and starts to press the pace. Someone else gets mad that the pace is increasing, and expresses the disgust by increasing the pace further until the last mile or two becomes an all-out race back to the school.

This can sometimes be good, when done on occasion or as a time trial workout. But often, runners or entire teams fall into a routine of racing workouts — or even racing easy days.

Some may feel that not being "first" in practice will result in mental weakness or a loser's mentality in a race. Some may feel the need to prove to themselves or their coach that they are in shape each day. Some may want to put a teammate in his or her place. Some may just get swept up in the excitement of a good chase.

Whatever the reason, regularly racing workouts is usually a path toward poor end-of-season performance. The main reason is that you're at high risk of wearing yourself out, and not being ready to race when it actually counts.

If you end up racing workouts a lot, have the courage and confidence to run at a more beneficial pace. You won't finish first in practice, but that was never the goal. The goal is to run your best at the races that count the most.

If you have trouble not racing in practice, use the same determination you have to finish first to set a firm goal of finishing behind a teammate who you know won't be going so fast.

## BREAK-THROUGH EXPERIENCES

There are few "nevers" and few "always" when it comes to running. If someone tells you to "always" or "never" do a certain kind of training, I can guarantee there's someone who does the exact opposite and runs great.

The concept of backing off is no exception. There are certain times when doing the opposite of backing off is best.

I spent a college quarter on a service-learning trip to the mountains of Guatemala. While there, I met a gentleman who was running intervals on an oval track that consisted of narrow footpath through the grass. With limited ability to communicate given my bad Spanish, we somehow agreed to meet at the track the next day for a run.

The next day, my guide led me at a jogging pace to a jeep trail that turned sharply upward and switchbacked 2,000 vertical feet up a lush ravine. We ran at a moderately brisk pace upwards for perhaps 20 to 30 minutes until the slope flattened. We jogged for a few more minutes on the flat to a collection of huts, then my guide signaled that we should turn around.

At this point, I was extremely thrilled to be "off the beaten track", and somewhat proud that I, the visiting gringo, was able to run a mountain road as well as a local. All that remained was the downhill part, and that would be easy.

We ran back to the edge of the ravine. My guide suddenly picked up the pace and yelled "Vamos!" After a moment of surprise, I took off after him at absolute top speed, feeling like I would go hurtling off the side of the ravine at the first switchback.

The jeep trail was eroded and rocky, but it didn't faze my guide in the least. I strained to keep up, while he gracefully put distance between us. After a few minutes, my legs were beginning to weaken, and my guide was so far ahead that I couldn't see him. I tried to slow down and control my pace, but the steepness of the road made this attempt futile.

At the bottom of the jeep road five minutes later, my insanely fatigued muscles felt like rocks of spasm and my leg bones felt as if they'd shattered in place. My legs buckled when I ran off the slope and onto the flat. My guide was waiting. Smiling and happy, the rocket ride down the mountain hadn't hurt him at all.

In the annals of what not to do, a sudden training session like this would top the list of great ways to get hurt and ruin your season. But it happened, and it absolutely blew my mind that something like this was even possible, let alone something that you could get comfortable doing. I had no idea that humans could go that fast in such conditions.

I thanked my guide and jogged slowly to my quarters. I couldn't walk for two days and my understanding of what's possible was forever changed.

Breakthrough experiences like this are often a part of learning the discipline of running. Maybe for you it's running your first 10-miler when your previous longest run was 4 miles. Maybe it's an unexpected 20-mile run when you meant to do 10. Maybe you find yourself suddenly keeping up with top varsity athletes on your team that you had long ago assigned to "god" status.

Whatever it is, there are times when backing off isn't right. Sometimes you find yourself in a position where you break through barriers of exhaustion, pain or belief — and go on to discover that you're capable of much more than you ever imagined.

I recommend that you stay open to these types of experience. But remember, these events aren't regular, day-to-day training. They're fairly rare events that maybe occur once or twice a year, or less often than that. Most of the time, it's best to utilize the concept of backing off — and training in a way that allows your body to adapt, thrive and feel good.

# TIP #14: BE SKEPTICAL OF STORIES ABOUT THE WAY OTHERS TRAIN

As a junior at Buffalo High School in Buffalo, Minnesota, my friend Jason Minnick was a successful miler looking for ways to up his game. Maybe even up his game to the level of Jim Kappel, a senior from Winsted, Minnesota, who was one of the top-ranked milers in the state.

The following year, as luck would have it, a boy moved to Buffalo from Winsted, where he had run with the great Jim Kappel. Again, as luck would have it, the boy joined the Buffalo cross-country team and told Minnick the secret to Kappel's success.

"You should see the guy's calves! They're huge. He does calf raises like crazy and walks around school all day up on his toes!"

So, during his senior year, Minnick began a calf-raise regimen and started walking around more on his toes. That spring, Minnick placed 5th in the mile and 4th in the 2-mile at the state track meet.

Must have been the calves!

The next year, Minnick was a freshman on the Mankato State University cross-country team. Who else was on the squad? Jim Kappel! It wasn't long into the cross-country season that Minnick told Kappel about how he had followed his calf-strengthening regimen.

"Calf raises?" Kappel scoffed. "I've never done any calf raises!"

## IT AIN'T NECESSARILY SO

If you're a runner, it's almost certain that you've curiously listened to stories about the training practices of other successful runners. And if you're a normal person, you've probably tried something new based solely on a story that you heard second or third hand. That's not always bad. Trying new things can be instructive and helpful.

Running your best — and maybe even becoming a great runner — can be tricky, fraught with lots of uncertainty, false starts and wasted efforts. Runners love to read or hear "how they train" stories, in part because they hope to unlock a secret or find the missing ingredient that will lead to success. I'm as guilty of this as anybody.

But whether it's a story about Jim Kappel or Kara Goucher or Ryan Hall, be careful about the conclusion you draw. Remember, just because someone allegedly trains in a certain way and is successful, it doesn't mean that:

* They did what they were reported to have done (or that it was anything more than a fragment of a larger plan)

* That was the key to their success

* It will work for you.

Most importantly, don't let stories of how others train erode confidence in the way you're training.

# TIP# 15: FOR ONE OFFSEASON, TRY RUNNING EVEN AMOUNTS DAY-TO-DAY

One of the most simplifying off-season training decisions you can make is to run even amounts on a day-to-day basis. This can be a hard concept to buy into as most runners are used to running a variety of durations during the week.

However, it's a great way for high school runners to stay focused on one of the absolute most important training tactics that will lead to improvement: that is consistently (and sustainably) putting in lots of quality miles over long periods of time.

Doing this means you start off choosing a distance or amount of time that you think you can run every day. If you're a beginning runner, that might be 1 or 2 miles (or 10 to 20 minutes) a day. If you're an experienced runner coming off a longer break, maybe you'd start at 3 to 5 miles a day (or 20 to 30 minutes).

## GETTING STARTED

When you select a duration, bear in mind that it's not what you can gut-out for one day or a few days. Rather, it's a duration that you feel you can run for many days — and perhaps weeks — in a row.

Once you have selected a starting duration, try running it for four days in a row. After four days, make an early judgment call on whether this distance is appropriate for you. If it feels way too easy, you may be able to add a mile a day to your duration. If it feels too hard, adjust the duration downward to something that feels sustainable.

Once you feel like you've arrived at a good daily duration of running, try to keep it up for two to three weeks. Once or twice a week, go 1 or 2 miles longer than the daily distance. These longer runs begin to prepare you for eventually raising your mileage level.

Some may derive confidence from trying not to miss a day. Others may find it beneficial to take a day off each week. Still, to stay true to the experiment, try not to take more than one day off a week (or perhaps 2 days off each week for a beginner), unless there's a good reason, such as being ill or injured.

Over the course of two to three weeks, you'll probably find that running your selected duration gets easier, and you may find yourself running faster over that duration without any additional effort, particularly if you also follow Tip # 16. Let it happen.

This is referred to as adaptation. Your body experiences a new stress and, so long as you can recover from this stress, your body will adapt and improve its ability to handle it — and even thrive off of it.

## INCREASING MILEAGE

After about two to three weeks of daily or near daily running of your first duration, you may feel ready to increase it — but you don't have to if you don't feel ready.

If you're a beginning runner doing less than 3 miles a day, adding a half-mile (or a few minutes) to each daily run may be enough. For a more experienced athlete running 4 or more miles a day, adding 1 mile (or six to eight minutes) to your daily duration is appropriate.

When you add mileage (or time), you'll probably feel fine for the first few days, then have a few days where your legs feel more fatigued than usual. If you can do your best to run through this fatigue as comfortably as possible the good feeling should return as your body adjusts and adapts to the new stress.

## THE ADVANTAGES

There are many advantages to this system for high school athletes who are still early in the process of discovering their body's capabilities. Here are a few:

* **Simplicity** — Once you pick a starting distance, you don't need to think about steps of advancement or an end level. The system is very easy to keep track of.

* **It keeps you honest** — A lot of people can run hard for a few days and then crawl off and disappear. When you know ahead of time that you'll need to run a certain duration every day, you're much more careful in selecting a duration and intensity of running that you know you can sustain over the long-term.

* **It reins you in** — Good runners with basic fitness can go a lot harder than their body is ready for — and they may be able to do this for a couple of weeks before the wheels start falling off. Consistent daily mileage can help prevent you from going too far too soon.

* **Consistency adds up** — A runner who starts running 3 miles a day on June 15 and conservatively increases the daily duration by a half-mile every two weeks will be at 5 miles a day by September. That means running 21 miles a week to start and 35 miles a week by summer's end. Sustainable, incremental advancement can quickly add up to some serious mileage.

* **Predictability** — When you run fairly consistently in duration each day, it becomes much more easy to predict how you're going to feel. You'll still have ups and downs, but it will be easier to identify causes of ups and downs because one of your major training variables isn't changing.

# TIP #16: FOR ONE OFF-SEASON, DISCOVER YOUR HIGH-END COMFORT ZONE

When it comes to daily mileage-type running that you'll be doing in the off-season, many high school runners stay within the easy end of the comfort zone.

That's not bad and is probably a good idea for beginners or for experienced athletes who are stretching their ability to run a lot of miles. In contrast, running during the regular season is often done at either the easy end of the comfort zone (for mileage or recovery runs), or at the 90 to 100% effort level.

What many runners miss out on is exploration of the middle ground between these two ends of the spectrum — namely the high-end comfort zone, which would be about a 75 to 88% (or roughly a 4/5ths) effort level. The "Spectrum of Intensity" chart on the next page can help you better understand what this means. Note that the ability to talk (or not talk) is one of the key indicators of intensity.

If you want to learn how to run fast, feel good and build confidence in your ability to train effectively, I would highly recommend that you spend time — off-season training is perfect — exploring the higher end of your comfort zone. This quest can be merged with the quest to run the same amount each day.

Sometimes, people who try this end up going too hard and realize within a few days that it simply isn't sustainable. If you feel really worn out after a few days of experimentation, you're probably going too hard and you'll need to dial back the intensity level. In fact, one way to target this level of training is to think to yourself during the run: "Could I do this again tomorrow?" If you don't think you could, it can be a helpful signal to slow down or reduce your effort level by a notch.

As you learn and practice running at a mid- to high-end comfort zone, you gradually adapt. You're likely to find that the pace you can comfortably sustain for a good portion of your daily run gets faster while the effort level stays the same — a major confidence booster. In addition, you begin to associate faster running with feeling good and feeling relaxed, which you can carry into in-season workouts and racing.

## SPECTRUM OF INTENSITY

| Low end Comfort Zone High end | | | Increasingly Uncomfortable | | |
|---|---|---|---|---|---|
| 5 to 15% effort level | 30 to 75% effort level (depending on distance run) | 75 to 88% effort level or 4/5ths effort level | 88 to 92% effort level | 93 to 99% effort level | 100% effort |
| Very slow and easy jogging. Usually for warm up or recovery. | Mid-level jogging, often associated with the long run. | Often considered a "tempo run" or "marathon pace" when done for distance. | Considered a "lactate threshold run" when done for 15 to 30 min. Can be done as intervals, too. | Associated with hard interval running. | This is race-type intensity. |
| Feels no harder than a walk. | This level only feels hard if you're feeling bad or have gone a long distance. | Should feel like a fast, effortless float. Out of five gears, you're in 3rd to 4th gear. | This nudges outside your comfort zone. You're probably in 4th gear, pushing to 5th. | Hard enough that for a portion of an interval you're struggling to maintain form, composure and speed. | All out, spent at the finish, gasping for air. You can't wipe the spit off your face. |
| No limits on ability to talk, even if you've gone a long way and are hurting in other ways. | | Once you're up to speed you should be able to say a brief sentence or two. In a group, talking noticeably diminishes. | Once you're up to speed you should be able to say no more than a few words. In a group, there's no talking. | Unable to talk except for one forced word or two. | |

## GETTING STARTED

Exploring your comfort zone involves starting out as you would with an ordinary fitness run where you start very slowly and gradually increase the pace over 10 to 15 minutes.

But instead of settling in at a low or medium comfort level, experiment with continuing to gradually increase to a significantly faster pace that doesn't require any straining or tension in your trapezius muscles (the muscles connecting your neck to your shoulders). Although running fast, your legs should feel light and be churning away at a fast, effortless float. The pace you run will vary depending on how you feel, but the effort level should stay the same.

Although fast, you should still be able to run in a light, relaxed way. Remember, you can always slow down or even stop for a minute to catch your breath if you feel like you're going over the line.

I'm quite experienced in running

*Tension starts in your trapezius muscles and spreads to the rest of your body. Continually assess the tension level of your trapezius muscles while running. When they feel tense, let them relax and melt down into your body.*

this way, and I stop briefly or slow down a little quite often. Usually it's because I'm feeling fast and having fun. I get carried away and need to dial back slightly to get back below a 90 percent effort level.

As you begin to map out the way higher-end comfort zone running feels — and the type of pace you can maintain and still feel comfortable — you can begin to spend longer and longer segments of your run within the high-end comfort zone.

## GIVE IT TIME

It will likely take a few weeks of consistent training to learn to listen to your body so that you can begin to accurately target this effort level. It also takes time to let your heart, lungs, tendons, muscles — every part of the running machine — gradually understand and adapt to their capabilities.

As you become more fit, you may be able to perform high-end comfort zone runs for numerous days in a row before you feel the need to take a rest day or easier day.

## COMFORT ZONE AND INTERVALS

High-end comfort zone running can also be used effectively when doing intervals. A shortcut to dialing in your high-end comfort zone during intervals is to simply back off a solid notch from your top effort level. Ask yourself during an interval: "Am I going at a 4/5ths effort level?," "Could I easily shift into a faster gear?," "Am I feeling fast, relaxed and light on my feet?"

If you spend time discovering your high-end comfort zone during the off-season, it'll probably be a lot easier to translate that feeling to more intense interval work during the in-season.

You may wonder: "How can I get fast if I don't run interval workouts all-out?"

A key concept here is adaptation. Intervals that you run in your high-end comfort zone don't always lead to instant results, but when performed over several sessions, you'll find that the pace you can run a particular set of intervals will get faster, while you remain at the same effort level.

When it comes to developing better speed, the answer isn't always just to go at a harder, faster effort in the hopes that your body's ability to adapt can keep up. Rather, you can shorten the length of your intervals until you can run at or near the desired speed and still be within the high-end comfort zone.

All-out intervals can sometimes play an important role in training. However, running intervals in your high-end comfort zone provides large and often untapped potential for improvement and adaptation that feels great and doesn't break you down.

## BONUS TIP: HOW TO COMBINE RUNNING THE SAME DAILY DISTANCE WITH COMFORT-ZONE RUNNING

The simplified chart shows that as your effort level stays fairly consistent you improve your running by gradually running more and by running faster. Of note: you deliberately choose your daily mileage and your effort level. You do not choose your pace. Your pace will come to you as you run in your high-end comfort zone, and is likely to get faster with no increase in effort.

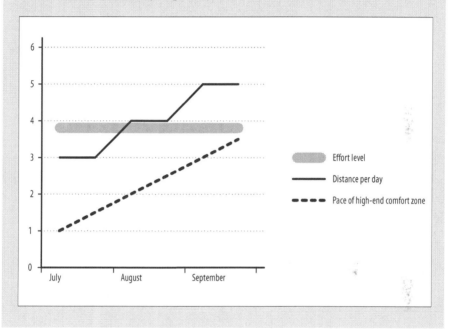

# PART III | HEALTH

Health issues can spoil everything, but there's a lot you can do to keep yourself healthy. Basic steps include getting proper sleep; eating a healthy diet; visiting a doctor when you have been ill for five days and aren't getting better (it may be appropriate to go sooner than that!); and minimizing stress and worry.

Do not gloss over the above points as obvious, no-brain things that you've got covered.

It is amazing to me how many people neglect the basic foundations of health, and then wonder why they don't feel right or are susceptible to problems.

I've done it myself. I once visited the campus doctor in college complaining of unusual fatigue that had lasted a long time. After discussing my situation and ordering a few tests, the doctor said that he thought that I probably needed more sleep. "But I try to get 7 to 8 hours a night," I replied. "Well," he said, "maybe you need more." The tests all came back normal, I got some more sleep, and what do you know, I felt better.

But let's get more specific.

# TIP #17: GET YOUR SERUM FERRITIN (IRON) LEVEL TESTED

In a 2009 position statement (viewable at *www.rungreatwhenitcounts.com*) the American College of Sports Medicine said that: "Athletes, especially women, long-distance runners, adolescents and vegetarians should be screened periodically to assess and monitor iron status".

Iron is important because it plays a crucial role in oxygen-carrying capacity. Iron is part of the molecule hemoglobin, which is the part of the red blood cell that carries oxygen. Lower iron levels can impair muscle function and limit your body's ability to work hard, which in this case means training and racing.

> *Correcting low iron stores can be a night and day experience for some people. Not only do some people race significantly better, but they also feel better when running and are much happier.*

A basic way to assess iron status is to have your serum ferritin levels tested. Ferritin is a protein that stores iron so that you body can use it later. When measured, it can give you an estimate of your iron reserves, which indirectly measures the amount of iron in your blood. It doesn't give a complete picture of your iron situation, but it can be a good early indicator of a potential problem.

Serum ferritin levels at the lower end of the normal range can severely impact your running performance. The "normal" range is 12 to 300 nanograms per milliliter (ng/mL) for men and 12 to 150 ng/mL for women. In other words, your serum ferritin test can be normal and your iron levels could be just fine for going about day-to-day life. However, researchers and coaches have noticed that the lower end of "normal" appears to be too low for endurance athletes. When you're running hard or racing and you have a great demand for oxygen, the low end of normal may be inadequate for good performance, let alone top performance.

Having iron levels that are low enough to impact your ability to run doesn't necessarily mean you have anemia. By definition, anemia is when your body reduces production of healthy, oxygen-carrying red blood cells, which can be caused by persistent or continued iron deficiency.

The main ways you can develop low iron levels are through consuming too little iron through diet to meet your body's needs — or loss of blood (internally or externally) that drains your iron stores over time. Vegetarians can be at higher risk of low iron levels because meat — particularly red meat — is a primary source of dietary iron. Girls and women are at heightened risk due to menstrual bleeding. Regularly giving blood could also heighten your risk of lower iron levels. Distance runners can have foot-strike hemolysis, which is when tiny blood vessels in your feet break from lots of foot-strikes on the ground, causing small amounts of blood to leak internally. There is also some iron loss in sweat. Even then, some people are likely more susceptible to developing low iron, and risk factors that lead one person to develop low iron may not cause low iron levels in someone else.

In the absence of a serum ferritin test, you may begin to suspect low iron stores if you have one or more of the following signs or symptoms:

* Your running performance plateaus for no known reason or even declines. It's common to start the season feeling good (when iron levels are adequate) then to feel worse as iron depletes as the season progresses. Note that performance plateaus or declines can happen even if your iron levels are fine.

* You've had a couple of good seasons or years where you ran great and felt good, but since then you've felt abnormally exhausted, your legs don't feel good, your performance has declined, your motivation level is down and your frustration level is high. For girls, this type of decline is common and it is often attributed to a "maturing" body.

* You start a race or workout feeling fairly good, but then after several minutes of continuous running, the running starts to feel harder than it should and you start to struggle. Your legs may feel heavy and your muscles tight. Many people view this as a struggle against mental weakness or as a lack of toughness. They assume that everyone feels the way they feel, but others are better able to tough it out.

* You tend to be unusually tired or exhausted from exercise. In the absence of exercise, you may or may not notice any unusual fatigue.

* You finish races or hard workouts with a pasty white pallor to the skin, especially of your face.

* You have lightheadedness or faint at the end of races or workouts.

These symptoms don't mean you should start taking iron supplements. They indicate the need for a serum ferritin test (and perhaps other tests your doctor may recommend) to determine if low iron may be part of the problem. You should never take iron supplementation without knowing your iron status. You should never start taking iron supplementation without consulting with a doctor. Serious problems can result from getting too much iron.

Once symptoms occur, it's probably a sign that your iron levels are very low. If you experience them mid-season, it's unlikely that you'll be able to rally and race your best by the end of the season. Even with careful, dedicated supplementation, iron stores can take months to improve — and if you're still training while supplementing, they may not improve much at all until you take a break.

Better than waiting for symptoms to develop is to have a serum ferritin test in advance of your competitive season. If your pre-season ferritin lev-

> *For more accurate results: Don't get a serum ferritin test when you are sick or injured as inflammation within the body can artificially raise serum ferritin levels. This can give you a "false positive" reading that's higher than it would normally be if you weren't sick or injured.*

els are good, testing at the end of a season can still be very instructive, because this will indicate where your iron stores are at after several months of hard training and racing.

If you've had a couple of serum ferritin tests with solid values, additional testing may become increasingly less worth the cost and hassle. Still, testing once or twice a year can be a good insurance policy against a problem that can be pretty sneaky.

## A FINAL THOUGHT

Correcting low iron stores can be a night and day experience for some people, although response to a plan to raise iron levels can vary. Not only do some people race significantly better, but they also feel better when running and are much happier. In addition, it has been my experience that a significant percentage of kids who are frustrated with the way they run in the latter half of a season have low iron levels. This is definitely an under-recognized problem among high school runners and it should be on everyone's radar screen.

Having said that, there are also many kids who are disappointed with the way they run at the end of the year who don't have low iron stores. Further, low iron stores may only be one piece of the puzzle. Correcting your iron doesn't make you super-human and give you license to neglect other aspects of your training and health that contribute to running your best.

## BONUS TIP: ADEQUATE FERRITIN?

Research has not yet determined a minimum threshold of serum ferritin that will not cause a decrease in performance. It has not even proved that low iron stores in the absence of anemia contribute to declines in performance (although some studies have suggested a link).

In the absence of hard evidence, many doctors think that serum ferritin levels that fall within the normal range and have not caused anemia are not a problem and should not be treated. Therefore, it may be hard to get your doctor to buy into the idea of even having a serum ferritin test, let alone giving you advice on how to treat lower ferritin levels, should you have them (see Tip #28).

Keep in mind that solid recommendations based on extensive research don't exist, but the chart below can provide suggestions for you and your doctor to consider. And again, do not take iron supplements without consulting with your doctor.

| SERUM FERRITIN LEVEL | DEGREE OF IMPACT | CONSIDERATIONS IN CONSULTATION WITH A DOCTOR |
|---|---|---|
| Above 55 ng/mL | None. This is the target level. | None. Test ferritin again at the end of season to measure a drop, if any. |
| 40-50 ng/mL | Mild to none, but there's little margin for further loss. | Consider upping intake of red meat or talk to your doctor about appropriate iron supplementation levels. Retest in 6 to 8 weeks. |
| 30 ng/mL to around 40 ng/mL | Likely noticeable and may slow you down | Talk to your doctor about appropriate iron supplementation levels. Retest in 6 weeks. May want to ease up on training. |
| Below 30 ng/mL | Likely to slow you down and potentially season-wrecking | Talk to your doctor about appropriate iron supplementation levels. Retest in six weeks. May need to limit or stop workouts harder than easy running. |

# TIP #18: GET ENOUGH CALCIUM AND VITAMIN D

Inadequate calcium intake (and/or inadequate vitamin D levels, since vitamin D helps your body use calcium) can increase your risk of low bone mineral density and stress fractures. When it comes to doing your best at the end of the season, nothing will knock you back like a six-week break as you wait for a stress fracture to heal. Lack of calcium and vitamin D isn't the only cause of stress fractures, but it can be a contributing factor.

You may think that little kids or little old ladies have the highest recommended daily allowance of calcium, but that isn't true.

Boys and girls between the ages of 9 and 18 have the highest recommended daily allowance (RDA) of calcium among all age groups, with an RDA of 1,300 milligrams of calcium daily. Calcium is important for growth, maintenance and repair of bone tissue. Although young children usually seem to drink plenty of milk, teenagers often gravitate away from it and instead choose water, Gatorade, soda or other beverages.

*Boys and girls between the ages of 9 and 18 have the highest recommended daily allowance of calcium among all age groups.*

Your best bet is to get adequate calcium through your diet such as by drinking milk or eating yogurt. An 8oz glass of milk or 1.5oz cheese chunk gives you about 300 mg of calcium. An 8oz yogurt is about 400 mg. A more comprehensive list of calcium content in foods and beverages can be found at *www.rungreatwhenitcounts.com*.

A great time for a carton of chocolate milk is within 30 minutes of finishing a run or workout. Not only do you get the calcium, but you also get electrolytes (sodium and potassium), carbohydrates (sugars) and protein that your body will quickly begin using to recover from exercise.

If you don't think that you get 1,300 mg of calcium a day — or if you don't get much sunlight, which is a source of vitamin D — talk to a doctor or nutritionist about how to get the calcium and vitamin D your body needs to be optimally healthy.

*Remember to drink your milk!*

# TIP #19: MAKE SURE YOU'RE TAKING ENOUGH STEPS

Barefoot running, foot gloves and minimalist shoes are all the rage. I don't wear them, but I'm not against them. Some people love the minimalist style, and that's just fine. The catalyst for their popularity is the idea that running in a typical cushioned training shoe leads many people to run with unnatural form, thereby causing uncomfortable running and increasing injury risk.

There's a certain amount of merit to this theory. However, you can usually correct this problem and gain the benefit of reducing injury risk without buying minimalist shoes or running barefoot.

Many beginning and intermediate runners do indeed run with an unnatural style (some experienced runners do, too). Their main fault is taking overly long strides that can result in a hard foot landing or a prominent heel-strike while running.

The modern cushioned running shoe can facilitate this problem. The cushion in those shoes allows people to land heavily on their heel or foot without causing intense and immediate pain. Still, the impact on your feet and legs is much higher with each step than with a lighter running style. Therefore, the more you run with a long stride and a heavy foot landing or heel strike, the more likely you are to develop pains and injuries.

The idea of barefoot or minimalist running is to make overly long strides and hard heel or foot striking so painful that you don't do it. If you try running barefoot down a sidewalk while landing with a heavy heel strike, you won't make it very far. Rather, you'll immediately adopt a quick, short stride in which you land gingerly on the ball of your foot, allowing the impact of striking the ground to be evenly and smoothly absorbed through the foot and leg. You'll also experience a similar situation when you run in a typical pair of track spikes with very minimal heel cushion.

This style of running causes much lower impact force on the foot and leg with each step than does a heavy heel strike (although there's still plenty of impact, especially if you're barefoot or wearing a shoe with little to no cushion).

But before you rush out to buy a pair of minimalist shoes, consider the fact that you can run with a long stride and prominent heel strike wearing minimalist shoes (at least, if you're running on something soft like on grass or woodchips) — and you can run with a quick, light stride wearing the foamiest, cushiest shoe on the market.

## IT'S HOW YOU RUN, NOT THE SHOE

The single best way to make sure you're running with more of a barefoot-like stride is to make sure you're taking enough steps. It's generally accepted that 180 steps per minute (or more) is the cadence that smooth, efficient runners adopt. Most experienced, competitive runners end up running in this way — and some beginners also do this straight away, as well. This cadence generally stays about the same whether jogging or running faster — even up to running 2-mile race pace.

To find out how many steps you take a minute, go for a run. After you've warmed into an easy, comfortable pace, time yourself for 30 seconds and count how many times your right foot hits the ground. Multiply that number by four, and you've got your answer. For example, if you count 41 steps, that's 164 steps a minute.

## TAKE QUICKER STEPS

If you're below 180 steps a minute, try taking quicker steps. It's that simple. You may want to think about letting your foot softly or lightly hit the ground or think about running on eggshells — or maybe if you're like Kristofferson in the movie Fantastic Mr. Fox, you'd try to feel "lighter than a slice of bread."

I would recommend not worrying about what part of your foot strikes the ground. When you adopt a quicker cadence, your foot will strike where it needs to. You may be a little more back on the heel, a little more toward you toes, or right on the midfoot. Try to let your foot land in a position that feels natural to you.

Experiment with quicker steps for 10 minutes and time your self again to see where you're at in terms of steps a minute. Some runners with a slow stride can lock right into a 180 step-per-minute cadence almost immediately. In others, it may take some time to get used to running with a quicker stride. In addition, it may take time for your muscles to adjust.

If you experiment with taking more steps a minute and it just doesn't seem right to you, remember, everyone's body is different and it's possible that taking 180 steps a minute (or more) just may not be for you. You never want to force something that doesn't feel natural, just because someone tells you it's right.

Similarly, 180 steps a minute isn't meant to be a rigid constraint. You'll take quicker steps when running really fast and possibly when running over bumpy terrain or up a steep hill. And, you may find times when slower steps or a prominent heel strike are warranted.

Overall, you can reduce the impact of each step you take while running (and thus reduce injury risk) by working toward taking at least 180 steps a minute. Take a few minutes on your next run to count your steps a minute and experiment with taking quicker steps if you're below 180 steps a minute.

# TIP #20: DON'T CARBO LOAD

It's become a tradition for many high school teams to have a pasta feed on the evening before certain races — especially the important ones at the end of the year. This tradition has been handed down from pre-race pasta feeds that occur before marathons. But here's the thing, a marathon is a lot different race than an 800-meter, 5K — or even a half-marathon or 25K race.

In a marathon, runners actually deplete their glycogen (stored carbohydrate) reserve because they are exercising for two or more hours continuously. Therefore, stoking up on carbohydrates the night before a race can add a little more glycogen to the system so that it takes you a little longer before you run out. However, there's a trade-off. The extra glycogen can make your legs feel a little heavy and may make you feel a bit sluggish for the first few miles of a marathon.

That's probably worth it for a marathon. But needless to say, if you have sluggish legs for the first few miles of a 5K, the race is over before you start to feel good. Moreover, there is no way that you'll run out of glycogen in a 5K or less, so having extra glycogen stored in your body is unnecessary.

So, you can go to the pre-race pasta feed and have fun, but just eat a normal amount of food. Don't stuff yourself with carbohydrates on the false theory that it will give you extra energy for the next day's race.

# TIP #21: USE MODERATION WITH HYDRATION BEFORE RACES

Hydration is an issue that captures a lot of attention. It's taken as fact that if you lose greater than 2% of your body weight to fluid loss, it compromises athletic performance. So, if you're like I was in high school, you carry around a water bottle all day at school and drink enough that you're visiting the bathroom between every class. On the day of big races, you may even drink more water just to make sure you're not dehydrated.

But the 2% rule isn't as sound as people think — especially for runners. The 2% rule has been fairly well documented in laboratory studies. This involves people riding on an exercise bicycle or running on a treadmill in a non-race setting.

However, studies of runners that look at an athlete's fluid loss and performance in outdoor racing environments — where they pace themselves to get to the finish line and drink as they feel they need it — come to a different conclusion. One study, published in the November 2011 issue of *British Journal of Sports Medicine*, found that people running a marathon who lost the most

*The idea that "you can't drink enough water" before a race isn't accurate.*

body weight due to water loss during competition ran the fastest. The people who lost 8% of their body weight during the race ran faster than those who maintained optimal hydration and lost less than 2% of body weight.

I'm not suggesting that you purposely loose water-weight before running a race — but the idea that "you can't drink enough water" throughout the day or before a race isn't helpful, either.

You may hear about people dying in a marathon because they drank too much water during the race. This is called hyponatremia and is caused by a rapid drop of sodium levels. Hyponatremia probably can't happen to high school kids who drink a lot of water and run a 5 kilometer race. Even if it doesn't, my personal experience suggests that drinking too much water leaves me feeling washed out and less ready to perform.

Even if that's not true for you, there's still absolutely no reason to drink more water than is needed to hydrate you. True, your body will get rid of extra water, but it can take a few hours before your body can process extra water and get rid of it.

## BONUS TIP: HYDRATION BEFORE A RACE

Here's what to do, according to the American College of Sports Medicine (find a link to its hydration position paper on *www.rungreatwhenitcounts.com*).

- For an afternoon race, drink 2-3 mL of fluid per pound of body weight during breakfast and lunch. Just for simplicity, use an old 12- to 16-fluid ounce pop bottle. This should mostly cover you and you'd probably be fine with only additional drinking fountain stops throughout the day or maybe an extra glass of water if you feel a little thirsty.

- For races that aren't in the afternoon, slowly drink 12- to 16-fluid ounces three to four hours before competition. This will probably mean that you drink this with a small meal or snack, which is good.

- Either of the above plans should give your body plenty of time to process the water and leave you optimally hydrated by race time. If you're urinating and the urine is fairly clear, you know you're doing just fine. If not, you may do well to slowly drink another 16 fluid ounce bottle two hours before the race.

- In the hours before the race, sips of water should be enough to quench any nervous thirst. You can even swish your mouth and spit the water.

- On really hot days or in really dry climates, it may make sense to drink more water if you feel thirsty. Other effective ways to beat the heat include keeping cool by staying in the shade and dumping water on your head.

In summary, use moderation when it comes to drinking water — or any other fluid such as Gatorade or Powerade. You don't want to be parched and thirsty before a race, but you don't want to be flooded with useless and potentially harmful excess water.

# TIP #22: BE WARY OF ABRUPT TRANSITIONS IN TRAINING

As discussed in Tip #2, injuries, illness and fatigue can gradually sneak up. But injuries can occur from more abrupt and obvious causes, as well. When this happens, it's most likely to occur due to abrupt changes in training type, volume or intensity.

What's tricky about this is that some people might get hurt with an abrupt change, and others might not. Or, an abrupt change might not cause a problem for you one time, but cause an injury another time. Or, you might get injured in the absence of an abrupt change.

If you want to play the best odds, be wary of abrupt changes such as these scenarios:

* You're a bit lazy over most of the summer, then you suddenly start running 5 miles a day as the summer ends or as the season starts.

* You're a beginning runner and have never done a sport before, then suddenly you're trying to keep up with other kids who have been in cross-country for two or more years.

*Don't strain to reach fitness. Always let the training come to you.*

* You take a well-deserved off-season break, but come off the break and jump back into training levels that are similar to where you left off.

* You've put in good off-season training, but you make a sudden shift to wearing spikes or running fast and hard on a track.

* During the first week or two of the season, you find yourself doing hard hill repeats, even though you haven't been running on hills much. Too much downhill running can also be a high-risk proposition if your body isn't accustomed.

Transitions are inevitable, but when you make one, consciously decide to hold back on the first few days or weeks that you try something new. Hold back to the extent that you don't feel like you're doing enough — and then gradually advance from there. Don't strain to reach fitness. Always let the training come to you.

## BONUS TIP: COOL TO HOT

In Minnesota, my home state, it's a springtime tradition for the weather to be chilly up until the week before the state track & field meet, and then switch overnight to 90 degrees and humid. The sprinters take off their parkas and rejoice, and the distance runners feel like they've been run over by a truck.

Transitions to hot weather are hard on the body. It's been my experience that it takes two weeks of running in hot weather before the body acclimates to a reasonable level — and many people never really get used to it. During the acclimatization period, you mostly feel like garbage while running, and more tired overall.

If the weather gets suddenly hotter within a week or two of your important races, try these tips:

- **Run less and run slower in training** — When it's suddenly really hot, I would unscientifically estimate that running is 30% to 40% harder on your body. If a heat wave hits, I would suggest backing off by at least 30% to 40%, particularly in volume, but also in the pace you run anything (other than, perhaps, limited amounts of short intervals).

- **Don't suntan** — It'll wear you out. This sounds like a no-brainer, but on a hot, sunny day, you'll find half the track team flopped onto the high jump pit soaking up the rays. When you run, wear sunscreen. This prevents the sun's radiation from damaging skin cells, which the body uses precious energy to repair.

- **Stay cool on race day** — Stay in the shade or air conditioning until the last possible second you need to be on the track. You may consider packing a gym towel with ice and keeping it to your chest while you wait for your race. Alternately, have a couple of gym towels soaking in ice water in a cooler, then wrap them around your shoulders and head. You don't want to be shivering or anything, but keeping your core body temperature from getting too hot is a key determinant of performance. If you forgot to plan ahead, douse your head and shoulders with cool water before you race. You may also consider abbreviating your warm up to reduce unnecessary heat gain. Just do enough to be loose and ready to run.

# TIP #23: DON'T RUN THROUGH PAIN

When it comes to injury, it's a challenge for runners at every level to know when a niggle is just a slight pain that will go away, or the start of something that will shoot you down.

My view is this: don't run through pain. Sure, some people are real whimps and will stop running at the slightest discomfort. Also, there may be a few problems that cause discomfort that decreases as you warm up or may not get worse with additional running.

However, pain is your body telling you that something is wrong. And it's best to fix a small problem quickly, rather than let it develop into something worse. Here's an idea of how to go about addressing pain:

## DAY 1

At the start of pain, stop and figure out what hurts. Try massaging the area and muscles connected to the area. Lightly stretch the problem area. Start back up at an easy pace and see if it fades and feels better.

If not, it's probably best to back off for the day. You may be able to run or jog at a pace that isn't aggravating. If the pain persists despite backing off, stop. Take the time to massage, stretch or ice the area in the hope that you'll feel better the next day. Also, be sure to tell your coach. She or he may be able to help you troubleshoot the problem and come up with ways to address it.

## DAY 2

Try easing into the day's run with some light jogging. If the pain is gone, that's great. You'll still want to be more gentle than usual, so as not to reactivate the pain.

If the pain is better but still there, take another easy-to-moderate day. Again, take the time to massage, stretch or ice the area in the hope of further improvement by the next day.

If it still hurts and there's little improvement in pain, take another day off running or just jog easy (if jogging doesn't hurt). You may consider visiting your school athletic trainer.

## DAYS 3 TO 5

Repeat the plan for day two. If by five days you're still having pain and it isn't getting better, it's probably time to see a doctor (see Tip #28).

# TIP #24: STRENGTHEN THE HIPS AND MIDDLE BUTT (GLUTEUS MEDIUS) MUSCLE

Do you have a knee that buckles inward when you run? Do you ever get knee pain that's related to your iliotibial (IT) band?

These are two common problems in runners. The main reason is that many runners don't use their side-to-side muscles much. All we do is move our legs in a linear front-to-back motion, with no cuts to the side (think soccer or basketball) no pushing off from the side (think ice skating), or backpedaling (think football defense).

Therefore, runners are classically weak in the small stabilizer muscle groups such as the gluteus medius.

## SIDE VIEW OF PELVIS AND HIP JOINT

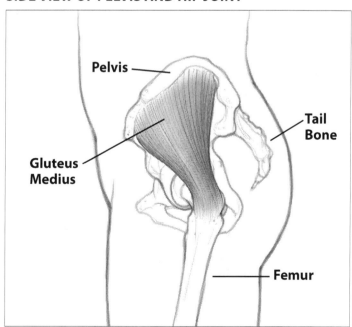

*The gluteus medius muscle attaches to the pelvis and the femur.*
*This is an important stabilizer muscle for the knee.*

Believe it or not, the middle butt muscle plays a large role in the stability of your knee. Your glute muscles more obviously are important to hip stability. Hip weakness causes the hip to buckle outward (as if you were giving someone a booty check) with each step. Watch any high school race and you will see dozens of kids with inward buckling knees and outward buckling hips.

There are probably a thousand good ways to strengthen the gluteus medius muscle and other stability muscles. But the exercises in the following pages can help take you a long way toward the goal of improving the function of your knee and hips.

These exercises or something similar are practically a "must" for any runner with wobbly knees or unstable hips. I would also strongly encourage just about any runner who doesn't also participate in a side-to-side sport such as basketball or hockey to do these, even if they don't have hip or knee issues.

If you look at photos of top high school runners sprinting to the finish in a race, you will often see hip or knee buckle. These athletes might not have this issue except under extreme stresses of a finishing kick. However, if you can become a little more stable and not have this occur even in a sprint, you'll lose less force to sideways buckle, which will then be applied to forward motion.

You'll get massive bang for the buck with these simple exercises that can be done very quickly and just about anywhere.

## KNEE STABILITY

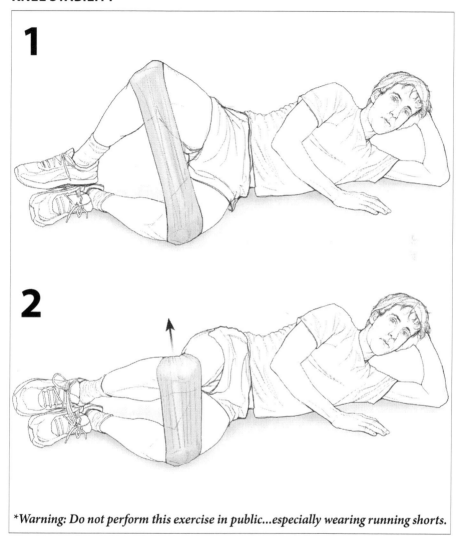

*Warning: Do not perform this exercise in public...especially wearing running shorts.*

### Clamshells

Lay on your side and bend your legs 90 degrees. Put an exercise band around both knees. Keeping your feet together, lift the upper knee so that your legs look like a clamshell. After you do enough to tire your middle butt muscle, flip over and work the other side.

This exercise takes one minute to perform. Done three times a week, it's a tiny investment towards avoiding knee pain and knee problems — not to mention running more efficiently.

## KNEE STABILITY

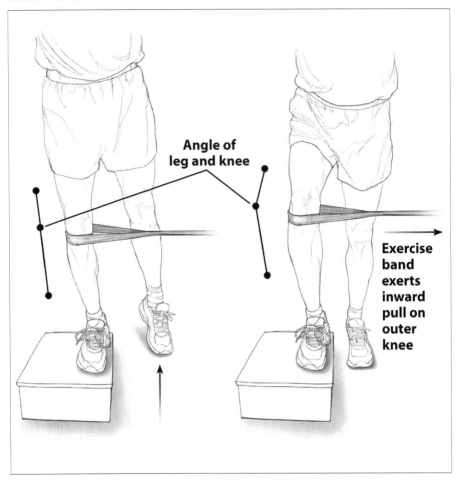

**Angle of leg and knee**

**Exercise band exerts inward pull on outer knee**

### Step ups against inward knee resistance

Find a stairwell. Tie an exercise band to the railing. Facing upstairs, stretch the band past the knee closest to the railing and wrap it around the knee farthest from the railing. The band should be able to pull your knee inward, just as it buckles when you run. With a fair amount of tension in the band, keep your knee straight and do a single step-up. Don't let the band pull your knee in. Repeat 10 times or so on each leg.

This brilliant exercise isn't so much for developing strength, it's more to get the nerves, muscles and other tissues firing and operating in the proper way.

## HIP STABILITY

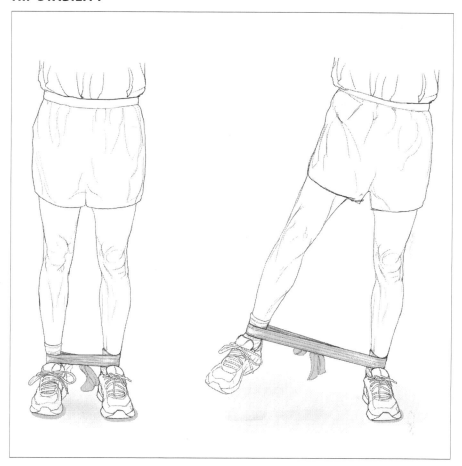

### Exercise band around the ankles

This is physical therapy 101. You tie off an exercise band in a circle and put it around your ankles. Try stepping side to side, or balance on one foot and stretch the other foot off to the side. Make sure to exercise both legs.

## HIP STABILITY

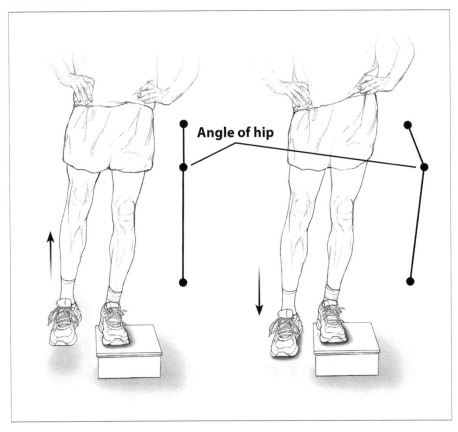

### Pelvis tilt on step or phone book

Stand sideways on a stair or phone book with one foot on the stair and one foot dangling off. Allow the foot that is dangling to drop about an inch or two. You should notice that your pelvis tilts to an angle. Lift the foot back to level in a way that also levels out your pelvis. Complete 10 or more repetitions and repeat on the other side. This is a particularly great exercise for improving IT band problems.

## HIP STABILITY

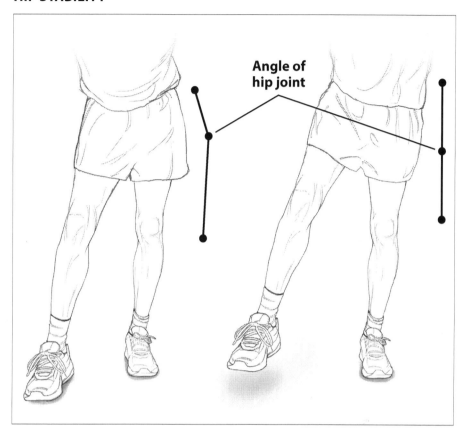

**Angle of hip joint**

### One leg balance with hip work

Stand on one leg. Jut out the hip of the leg you're standing on, then pull your hip back in so that there is vertical alignment going up your leg and through the hip. Repeat in a slow, controlled manner until you feel a little burn. Then switch legs and do the same thing. An alternate way to do this isometrically is to just stand on one leg and hold the position in which your legs and hip are vertically aligned. Save time in your day by doing this while also doing another task such as brushing your teeth or standing in the lunch line.

# TIP# 25: KEEP WEIGHT TRAINING AND CORE WORK IN PERSPECTIVE

Many athletes assume that strengthening — particularly core strengthening — will make them better runners.

In the annals of running history, some incredibly fast runners have made gym strengthening a major part of their training. Other incredibly fast runners have done virtually no gym strengthening. Therefore, it's hard to make any definitive recommendation on what's best.

My short answer is this: some is good, a lot isn't better. The main way to become a better runner is to run. Any role that weight training and core exercises play in running better is supportive, not central.

But that support is often important in two main ways:

## AS A SUPPLEMENT TO HILL RUNNING IF YOU DON'T DO MUCH OF IT

When it comes to improving performance, you need to be strong to run well. By merely running, you strengthen the appropriate muscles, which includes the core muscles that keep you upright. If you run on hills, you're strengthening your muscles even more. Running hills is the mode of strength building that the East African athletes generally take.

Running hills is a dynamic, sport-specific strengthening exercise and can be done in many ways, such as by running short, steep hills for all-out power, or long, lower-grade hills for more endurance-related strength. Plyometric jumping and bounding exercises on hills can be another dynamic, sport-specific way to add strength and agility. If your coach has you running a lot of hills or doing other hill work, you may not need much additional strengthening work to run your best.

If you're not doing much hill work, consider doing some leg strengthening exercises such as squats, dead lift or lunges and calf raises — but you don't need to do a lot or be maxing out. Try two to four sets a week of 12 repetitions or fewer. The exercise should feel challenging by the last repetition, which may be enough for good baseline strength without over-doing it. Plyometric jumping and bounding exercises can be a more dynamic way to add strength, even if not done on hills.

## FOR PREVENTING INJURY

When it comes to injury prevention, gym strengthening can increase the support that muscles and tendons give to bones and joints. It also increases you body's ability to absorb shock.

Strengthening may be of particular benefit if you have weakness that's leading to bad body mechanics. The exercises in Tip #24 are directed common problem areas, but you may have other weak, unbalanced areas that would benefit from strengthening.

In addition, general strengthening that involves the core trunk area and, to a lesser extent, the upper body is usually helpful. Lots of teams do group exercises like sit-ups, planks, push-ups, pull-ups and other supplemental exercises. Throwing around a medicine ball happens to be one of my favorites.

Group exercises, plyometrics and some weightlifting can be of benefit in terms of performance and injury prevention. Still, you should keep this role in perspective. The ability to do 10 push-ups or even 100 — or putting up 400 pounds on the squat rack — isn't going to be the main factor in how fast you can run.

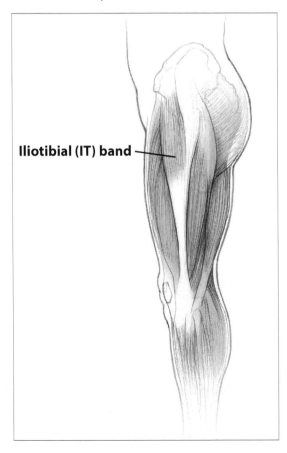

**Iliotibial (IT) band**

*Runner's knee is a common injury involving the iliotibial (IT) band that occurs on the outside of the knee. Strengthening stabilizer muscles of the hips and butt, being evenly flexible and gradually increasing mileage and intensity can help reduce your risk of developing runner's knee and other knee and hip problems.*

# TIP #26: BE EVENLY FLEXIBLE

Are you so flexible that you can trim your toe nails with your teeth? Or, are you so inflexible that your fingertips will sooner ring the doorbell at the White House than touch your toes? When it comes to running, success doesn't seem too dependent on your flexibility. I'm not anti-stretching; it helps me limber up and avoid injury. But I'm not sure that it makes me a better runner, except to the extent that it might prevent an injury.

When it comes to avoiding injury, the key consideration with flexibility is being symmetrical. That means having muscles on corresponding sides of the body being similarly flexible.

For example, having one quadricep that's tighter than the other — or having quadriceps that are less flexible than your hamstrings — leads to imbalance. This increases stress to joints, tendons, muscles and other tissues on one side of the body. It's a subtle effect — you may not feel imbalanced — but when people complain of a problem on one side of their body, it can often be traced to an imbalance of flexibility or strength.

This may be especially true with patellofemoral pain (felt as pain on the underside of the patella, which is often related to tight quadriceps) or IT band syndrome (See Tip# 24).

Static stretching (stretching a muscle and holding it for 30 seconds or so) performed when you're still warm and loose after exercise on each of the major muscle groups is a good way to achieve and maintain symmetry. If you find any imbalances, spend extra time gently stretching the less flexible muscles each day, with the goal of evening out flexibility over time.

# TIP# 27: GIRLS: IF YOU'RE NOT HAVING YOUR PERIOD, SEE A DOCTOR

Active girls who are driven to excel in sports are at risk of developing the female athlete triad of an eating disorder (not eating enough or purging), cessation of menstrual cycle and bone-weakening osteoporosis.

The triad often begins as disordered eating and involves dieting and additional exercise that go beyond ordinary training in the hope of losing (or maintaining) weight and being thin. Inadequate nutrition, excessive training and possibly other diseases may cause you to stop having your period. If you haven't had your period by age 16, have missed three consecutive periods or have your period at intervals greater than 35 days you need to be seen by a doctor. Missing your period doesn't mean you have the female athlete triad, but it's a sign of a potential problem, particularly that of developing bone thinning and osteoporosis in both the near term and later in life.

The female athlete triad is a serious health problem independent of running or athletics. When it comes to running, the triad leaves you low in energy, increases your risk of injury (particularly stress fractures), delays recovery, can cause anemia, impairs your coordination, dehydrates you and leads to declining performance in athletics and academics.

The bottom line is this: if you're not having your period, see a doctor.

There is a link to a nice brochure on the female athlete triad developed by the American College of Sports Medicine at *www.rungreatwhenitcounts.com.*

## TIP #28: FIND A DOCTOR WHO IS A RUNNER OR WELL-VERSED IN ENDURANCE SPORTS

Visiting a non-athletic doctor for an athletic issue can be a frustrating experience. A doctor may not understand why you want a serum ferritin test if you feel o.k., or may recommend "no running" as a way to make a treatable running injury go away. A family doctor sees a parade of sick, aged, unhealthy and deconditioned people all day: it's no surprise that he or she may not give good advice for an athletic problem. You aren't 200 pounds overweight with worsening heart failure, what are you worried about?

However, you're trying to make your body perform at its best, not merely seeking to avoid disease, discomfort or death.

Of course there are doctors who aren't athletes but who are great at treating sports problems. If this describes your family doctor, stick with him or her. Otherwise, if you want a doctor who is more fully aligned with what you're trying to do, find a doctor who is an endurance athlete (preferably a runner), a past endurance athlete — or at least a doctor who is athletic.

# PART IV | TALENT

Talent can take many forms. There's the obvious physical talent of athleticism. Work ethic is also a talent. Sound judgment is a talent. So is motivation. Most talent is innate; though some is developed. The very best runners have the full package, but most of us have weaknesses.

Generally, you get what you were given and talent is the factor that you can do the least to alter. Since your physical talents aren't going to change, the best next step is to be honest with yourself about what they are.

# TIP #29: UNDERSTAND YOUR TALENT LEVEL

Understanding your talent level can help you develop realistic expectations and align your training with the reality of who you are. This can greatly facilitate satisfaction. Don't worry about limiting yourself with realistic expectations because you can always exceed your expectations when it counts the most.

Below are three major tiers of talent:

## THE RECREATIONAL GROUP

When it comes to running fast, some people, no matter how hard they work, will only be recreational runners. That's o.k. I tried very hard as a young man to be a musician, but no matter how much I practiced (and I practiced a lot), I just didn't have it. That's the way it goes. Music still brings a lot of enjoyment and satisfaction to my life; I'm just not the person on stage.

If you can't keep up at a competitive level, but still want to run, non-competitive goals such as health, fitness, self-betterment or making friends can lead to tremendous satisfaction as a runner. If you're frustrated with your ability, consider other avenues of fitness and competition that better suit your physical talents. Think about it: the majority of athletes competing in the Summer and Winter Olympics probably aren't very good runners — but they are among the best in the world in their chosen discipline.

## THE "HARD WORK PAYS OFF" GROUP

There are a lot of runners with good to really good (but not great) talent who find that consistent hard work pays off in terms of success. They also get the benefit of having fun, being fit and making friends. Runners with average or above-average talent who can train consistently and appropriately — while staying healthy, fit and out of trouble with the law — can beat more talented runners, especially over the long term. In fact, it's often the case that the star high school distance runners don't do well in college, while good-but-not-great high school runners see their work ethic and consistency blossom in college and beyond.

Just as a reality check, however, it isn't likely that someone of above average talent will outperform someone with top talent who has a similar level of discipline, motivation and work ethic.

## TOP TALENT

If you're a highly talented athlete, that's great. Things might come easy at first. But as many an exasperated coach will attest, some athletes with tremendous athletic talent don't have the ability to work hard or have the motivation to compete or even participate. Further, relatively easy success in early years seems to stunt the ability to work hard or rebound from setbacks in many athletes, therefore limiting long-term improvement and success.

Don't expect anything big if your physical talent isn't coupled with smart, consistent training. On the other hand, smart, consistent training can lead to results that most people couldn't achieve even if they did similar training. The cold, hard reality is that only people with top talent (I wasn't one of them) have the ability to be among the best American runners. If you have it, I hope you make the best of it.

And don't forget to enjoy good health, fitness, making friends, having fun and other sources of satisfaction that go beyond running performance.

# PART V | LUCK

Ah, luck: the secret fifth element of successful running. As my college coach Mark Schuck always said: "You've got to be good, and a little bit lucky." Sometimes everything goes right and you win the race or destroy your nemesis — and it feels easy. Other times, despite your best efforts, bad things happen or you just don't quite have it when you want it most.

Assuming that there's nothing amiss, about the only thing you can do about Lady Luck is be grateful and enjoy the moment when she shines on you…and smile and say "better luck next time" when she doesn't.

Although you can't control your luck, I think you can still do a better job of using luck to your advantage.

By the way, that's me in the photo above. I'm in high school, having good luck. Sure, I got beat at the line by rival Pat Hoard, but it was a great race and Pat was a great runner and a tough competitor. Plus, this photo was on the front page of the StarTribune sports page — above the fold and above a significantly smaller picture of Joe Montana.

Now that's good luck!

# TIP #30: "EIGHTY PERCENT OF SUCCESS IS JUST SHOWING UP"

This tip is another quote from Coach Schuck. The next 10% of success is "stay awake," and the final 10% is "put forth a little effort." There you have it, a recipe for 100% odds of success.

This is a lesson I learned in 10th grade. In the fall of that school year, I didn't participate in any after-school activity. I didn't want to get beat up in football, I'd never played soccer and running cross-country sounded like torture. My only plan was to shoot some hoops to get ready for the basketball season. I knew I wouldn't get bored because my friend Bob had Nintendo and cable television, and it was fun to goof around at his house between the time that school ended and his parents returned from work.

Trouble was, Bob joined soccer. So did Pete. Ted was in a play. Dennis moved to a different city. I'd just come home from school and ride my bicycle around, checking the usual places to see if anyone was around. No one was. My chances of success — or even just making friends and having fun — were pretty much zero because I hadn't bothered to show up.

If you're reading this book, chances are you've already decided to show up — and have probably stayed awake and put forth effort. Good for you. Not everyone does. Maybe you won't be a superstar runner, but the habits you learn in track and cross-country are likely to carry on to other endeavors, and you'll probably be a healthier and happier person because you learned how to exercise. That sounds like success to me.

If we focus just on running performance, the idea of "showing up" is more than just deciding to go out for track. Showing up extends to the ideas discussed in Tip #1 — namely running most days. If you "show up" with near-daily running — whether it's showing up on your front step by yourself for your daily run, or showing up for an organized practice — you put yourself in a position for success and luck to happen.

You can't win the lottery if you don't buy a ticket, and it's impossible to have the magical "lucky" race if you don't show up and put forth a little effort.

# TIP #31: KNOW IF IT'S BAD LUCK OR SOMETHING ELSE

The two lines of thinking with this tip revolve around how you felt at the race, namely:

### "I FELT GOOD BUT DIDN'T GET THE RESULT THAT I WANTED"

If this bothers you, it can be a problem. It's hard — if not impossible — to feel brilliant and run extraordinarily great on cue. This can be an especially puzzling realization for runners who have an amazing "outlier" result, then wonder why they can't do it again. If you always expect brilliance, you're likely to be disappointed most of the time.

Even if you don't finish where you wanted, feeling good means you had good luck — maybe not extraordinary luck, but certainly not bad luck. When you feel good, chances are you'll be running at least on par with what you normally would run. If you do this at big races most of the time, you're experiencing more success than you may realize. Another one of Coach Schuck's frequent sayings: "If you run nationals the same way you ran regionals, you'll be an All-American." He was almost always right.

I'm not suggesting that you should settle for mediocrity, avoid dreaming big or hold back from "going for it" in a big race. However, lofty expectations for how you might possibly run if the stars properly align often makes it hard to do well at the end of the season.

For example, you may insist on running the early splits of a race too fast because you think that that's where you should be, even though you're not. Or you may train beyond yourself (i.e. at too high of intensity or volume than your body is ready to accept) in a sort of all-or-nothing, "Hail Mary" attempt to give it your all or go down trying.

Most go down trying.

Those who don't totally go down usually don't do any better than if they'd just trained in a more moderate way — and they're a lot less happy and more likely to get hurt. In fact, you can often predict when someone is likely to have a lousy goal race when you hear that they're doing incredibly hard and amazing training.

Rather than train beyond yourself in the hopes of unlikely brilliance, try training in a way that keeps gradually raising your "par" (See Tip #3). Having a par that rises each year is an incredible achievement. It sets you up for consistent high-quality performance for most races, yet you're still poised to take advantage of the brilliant days in which you have amazingly great luck.

## "I FELT BAD, AND MY REGULAR COMPETITORS WERE WAY AHEAD OF ME"

Bad luck can happen, but it's important to differentiate between an unlucky result and a result due to a training scheme that isn't working or a health issue. Feeling merely good-but-not-brilliant on the day of a big race may just be a matter of luck. Feeling bad or empty on the day of the big race is more likely to mean something wasn't right. Also, a repeated pattern — good or bad — is probably not due to luck.

For many of my high school and college seasons, I routinely hoped for a break-through race to occur at the most important races of the year — something similar to what happened to me at the race mentioned in the foreword of this book. Aside from that great race, it seldom happened, and sometimes I had the worst race of the season at the end.

But through all of those years, I failed to realize that bad luck wasn't the main prob-lem. Something about my training needed to change. Instead, I did more of the same — I worked too hard and hoped for better luck during the next season.

Most of the tips in this book are meant to help you avoid repeatedly grinding through training that isn't leading to the results you know you're capable of achieving. When a disappointing end-of-season occurs, I hope you take time to consider the all of the tips in this book to start along the path to discovering what works best for you.

# PART VI | SO WHAT SHOULD I DO?

I once consulted with a young woman who had just wrapped up an injury-plagued senior track season — and was hoping for something better in college. During the two-hour visit, I felt that I'd discussed many of the main points that would likely help her improve in the future. A day later, I got an e-mail that asked: "So, what am I supposed to do?"

If you're wondering the same thing, start by completing or implementing the tasks listed on the following page and checking off the boxes when it's complete.

If you've had trouble running your best at the most important races of your track or cross-country seasons — whether it's because you always seem to get injured or you feel worn out or stale — taking these few steps represent some of the greatest gains you can make in terms of turning your direction around and setting a foundation for future success.

Once you've implemented these major steps, continue to refine your training approach and philosophy with other tips in this book — and by experimenting with what works for you with a clear-eyed focus on the results of what is happening, rather than what, in theory, is supposed to happen.

If you're still having trouble figuring where to start or where to focus, contact me through my website: *www.rungreatwhenitcounts.com*. I offer reasonably priced consultations to help guide you through a critical analysis of your training habits and approach to running — then I help you define prioritized steps you can take to improve your ability to run your best when you want to.

## "SO, WHAT SHOULD I DO?" — THE CHECKLIST

☐ **Run most days** (Tip #1), unless you have reason not to such as being sick, taking a needed break, or being in another sport. Stay focused on consistently (and sustainably) putting in quality miles over long periods of time.

☐ **Start at a level you can easily handle and build on that**, whether you gradually add volume (mileage) or gradually add speed, or both (Tips #2 and #3). The key term here is "adaptation."

☐ **Get your serum ferritin tested (Tip #17), and possibly get other iron-related tests your doctor may recommend.** This step may also involve finding a doctor who is either a runner, well versed in endurance athletics or at least willing to be receptive to your desire to address issues related to training for running (Tip #28).

☐ **Get even...with strength and stretching, that is.** Test your major muscle groups to see if they are evenly strong and evenly flexible. (Tip #26). Take action to address imbalances in flexibility or strength. For example, consider strengthening stabilizer muscles of the hips and knees to promote further evenness of your body mechanics (Tip #24)

☐ **Take a few minutes on your next run to count your steps per minute.** Experiment with taking quicker steps if you're below 180 steps per minute (Tip #19).

☐ **Experiment at least a few times with making a conscious decision to back off during harder efforts**, particularly by backing off to more of a 4/5ths effort on days when you feel good (Tip #13). If this seems to work for you, consider backing off a notch on a routine basis — or consider making high-end comfort zone training a regular part of your training strategy (Tips #4, #7 and #16).

## ACKNOWLEDGEMENTS

My sisters Lynn and Patti — and Paul Rohde — provided indispensable mega-help with copyediting, layout and design. Michael King saved the day with the illustrations. Chip Cheney, Kraig Lungstrom, Christel Richter, David Sorenson, Tish Torchia and Jarrin Williams took time to provide sweet photos for this book, and asked nothing in return. Aleta Capelle, Chris Frye, Greg Hexum, Michael Joyner, M.D. and Greg Sorenson generously offered assistance with editing and feedback. Nothing can be done without the love and support of my lovely and talented wife, Chersten. And there's Lilly and Jon who do a great job of helping me stay young. Thanks to all for helping me make this dream a reality.

## ABOUT THE AUTHOR

**Joey Keillor** ran cross-country and track at St. Louis Park High School in St. Louis Park, Minnesota. In his first race — 400 meters on the track — he spent the first 375 meters self-consciously adjusting his running shorts, which felt too small. In subsequent years, Keillor participated once in the Minnesota state cross-country meet, twice in the Minnesota state track and field meet, and once in the Minnesota state cross-country skiing meet. Keillor later ran at Minnesota State University, Mankato, where he was a seven-time Division II All-American and national champion in the steeple-chase. Since then he has competed on the roads, track and trails, at distances ranging from 1 mile to the marathon. For the past decade, Keillor has been Associate Editor of *Mayo Clinic Health Letter*, a newsletter dedicated to health, fitness and wellness of older adults. In 2011, he started Joey Keillor Coaching, a consulting business dedicated to helping people run fast, feel good and train effectively without wasting time.

Made in the USA
Charleston, SC
15 July 2012